T0095475

Who's to Blame?

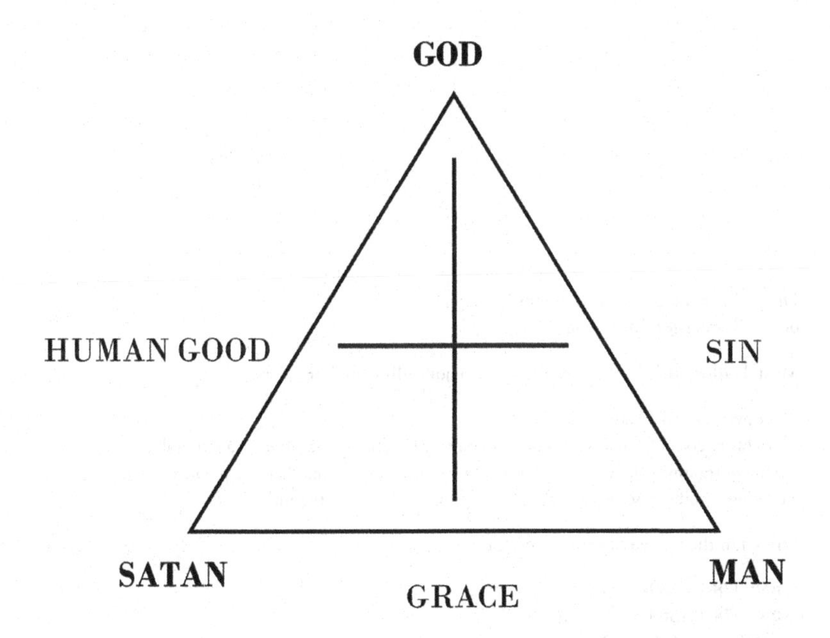

Kali Molefi

Order this book online at www.trafford.com
or email orders@trafford.com

Most Trafford titles are also available at major online book retailers.

Printed in the United States of America.

ISBN: 978-1-4669-5793-0 (sc)
ISBN: 978-1-4669-5791-6 (hc)
ISBN: 978-1-4669-5792-3 (e)

Library of Congress Control Number: 2012916942

Trafford rev. 01/16/2013

www.trafford.com

North America & international
toll-free: 1 888 232 4444 (USA & Canada)
phone: 250 383 6864 • fax: 812 355 4082

What I feared has come upon me, what I dreaded has happened to me. Now I have no peace, no quietness; I have no rest, but only turmoil.

(Job 3:25, 26)

Contents

Acknowledgments

This book is dedicated to those who need the grace, mercy, love, and faithfulness of God. I thank my lovely wife, Mmatsonelo Molefi, for giving me the support and encouragement to write this book from my heart and furthermore for giving me the space to do so. I thank my three kids, Tsoanelo, Thato, and Kamohelo, for being a source of inspiration and motivation in writing this book. I acknowledge the late Pastor Robert B. Thieme Jr. (pastor of Berachah Church, Houston, Texas) for teaching us the Word of God from original languages of scriptures in light of historic context and its relevance today. Furthermore, I thank the whole congregation of Berachah Church in Houston, Texas, for freely making it possible to the world to get such teachings free of charge.

I thank my brothers- and sister-in-law, Mochekoane, Matsita, Junior, and Lennox, for exposing and introducing me to Pastor Robert B. Thieme Jr.'s teachings.

Dear Reader,

As I was writing this book, I had you, my family, and my friends in mind because you still have a chance to turn back to God or accept Christ as your Lord and Savior if you have not done so.

I have sinned against my God with my thoughts, my behaviors, and my tongue. My life is in God's hands, and he alone will decide my fate.

However, my intention is to give you hope and encouragement to learn from my mistakes and foolishness in order to change and save your own life while you can by accounting and taking responsibility for your own faults, understanding Satan's tactics and God's permissible will in your life.

By the time you finish this book, your life will never be the same as you would have been challenged to think, take account, and see the grace, mercy, and faithfulness of God in your own life.

This moment will never come again, and as you read, may you see the hand of God at work in your life for Christ's sake, and may you find peace, quietness, and rest.

Yours faithfully,

Kali Silence Molefi

Introduction

We all have our lives to live and one being different from the other, but we all go through the same facets of life. The focus of this book is to know why do we suffer, who is responsible, can you overcome it and if yes, how? The book explores human solutions, feelings, reactions, and pieces of advice in dealing with crisis in our lives and compares human view point with what the Word of God says about your situation and divine solutions.

This book encourage believers or Christians_to be true to themselves and evaluate whether their suffering is due to their wrong decisions or Satan or God allowing suffering in their lives for their own growth, blessing, and discipline. The book is written in a dialogue form to allow two characters who represent the human view point during suffering in comparison to the divine view point (Bible) during suffering. The book further shows the difference between religion and Christianity and the fact that they are not one thing. The author is pushing the readers, whether they are believers or not, to come to terms with the fact that while on earth, suffering will come their way to either discipline or bless and more than once.

The theme of this book is that suffering is here to stay and faith in Christ alone is the only solution. This book teaches that Satan brings suffering in our lives to try to move us from serving, fearing, and trusting our God and the very God allows the same suffering in order to discipline or bless us right under the devil's nose. The author shows us that Satan attacks us in the most important areas of our lives: our family, our wealth, and our health. The stories of Job and the prodigal son are used as a foundation of this book and are dedicated to those who need Christ as their savior and those who already have Christ but seek the truth, peace, quietness, and rest in the midst of all their suffering, past, present, and future, and he wishes them as readers to see the hand of God at work in their lives.

Two characters are used to represent both the human and God's view point in a crisis. Tumelo (faith) represents a student of the Word of God expressing his frustrations and human view point, and Karabo (answer/solution) represents a pastor or teacher expressing God's view point in the Bible.

Chapter 1

Misfortunes

Pastor Karabo: Good evening, Tumelo.

Tumelo: Good evening, Pastor Karabo.

Pastor Karabo: I have not seen you in church in two years. Where have you been?"

Tumelo: Moving here and there with no hope, direction, or interest in life.

Pastor Karabo: What happened, my son?

Tumelo: Life happened, Pastor, life happened!

Pastor Karabo: Do you want to talk about it?

Tumelo: It's a long story, and I don't want to bother you with my problems.

Pastor Karabo: Maybe I can help!

Tumelo: No one can help, Pastor.

Pastor Karabo: You talk like a person who has little faith in God.

Tumelo: Faith in God! What's the point? The very God is responsible for my misery.

Pastor Karabo: Surely you are hurt, my son!

Tumelo: I'm devastated, Pastor, I'm destroyed. God has turned against me, and I have no peace, no quietness. I have no rest but only turmoil."

Pastor Karabo: I see you quote and relate your story to that of Job! Then we need to go back to basics.

Tumelo: I don't need a lecture! I'm tired. I'm drained.

Pastor Karabo: What you need is not a lecture but the truth! I see you are in a hurry now Come to the church office tomorrow, and let's talk and see what the Word of God has to say about your situation.

Tumelo: I don't promise, Pastor, but I will try.

Pastor Karabo: Don't try, Tumelo! Do it!

Tumelo: See you then tomorrow at 10:00 a.m.

Pastor Karabo: Confirmed.

Tumelo: Good night, Pastor.

Pastor Karabo: Good night, my son!

Tumelo: Pastor Karabo, before I go, what do I need for tomorrow?

Pastor Karabo: Just yourself. You have to tell me your story in full, what went wrong, why is it that you blame God.

Tumelo: See you!

NEXT DAY:

Pastor Karabo: Tumelo, it's only 8:45. You are early, but great, we start a little bit early.

Tumelo: I can come back at 10:00. It's just that I could not sleep, reflecting on what has happened to me and my family.

Pastor Karabo: Then you have made the right decision. There is a lot of work ahead of us. Tea or coffee?

Tumelo: Water will do.

Pastor Karabo: Only water? Are you health conscious?

Tumelo: I have to take care of my health. I have been sick latterly: neck pain, pain behind, above, and inside my right ear. It's so unbearable.

Pastor Karabo: Possibly stress! Why don't you go to the doctor?

Tumelo: I fear the worst: possible stroke, heart attack, or brain cancer. I would rather not know and just wait for my time.

Pastor Karabo: You are being irresponsible! What if you can be helped? What if it is not as bad as you think, and even if it's what you suspect, who says you can't be helped?

Tumelo: Let's get to today's business. Where do we start?

Pastor Karabo: From where it all started up to now.

Tumelo: Let me start by saying I knew that this day will come where God has turned his back against me and all going wrong.

Pastor Karabo: How so?

Tumelo: While all was well swimming in the pool of success and wealth, it became difficult for me to serve God, study his words, put him first in my life and in everything I did! And because of this, I lived with guilt and fear that one he will take it all and make me pay.

Pastor Karabo: So! That's why you are blaming him for your misfortune?

Tumelo: Of course, who should I blame? Satan?

Pastor Karabo: How about you, yourself?

Tumelo: What do you mean me? Are you blaming me?

Pastor Karabo: Let's not deviate or jump the gun! We'll discuss who to blame, but for now, I listen to your story.

Tumelo: OK, I will start.

Pastor Karabo: Before you start, let us pray for guidance. Heavenly Father, we thank you for this opportunity to reflect and seek answers from your word so that we can find the truth and make sense of our challenges. Amen.

Tumelo: One morning I took my car for a normal service. I dropped the car at the dealer around 9:00. At 12:00 noon I received a call from the dealer asking me to call the tracking company that I use to try a trace my car as my car has just been stolen at the dealer few minutes ago.

Pastor Karabo: Then what did you do?

Tumelo: I immediately called the tracking company, who then alerted the police of the stolen car, a white Dodge Nitro, a beautiful, aggressive machine.

Pastor Karabo: From the way you describe your car, I can tell you loved it.

Tumelo: I adored the machine, with no scratches, dents and had low mileage.

Pastor Karabo: Do you want another glass of water?

Tumelo: Please, Pastor! Where was I?

Pastor Karabo: Tracking story . . .

Tumelo: An hour later the trackers and the police told me they have lost the trail. The thieves must have removed and destroyed the tracking device.

Pastor Karabo: Sad news. Did you open a case?

Tumelo: The dealer manager had already opened a case on my behalf since the incident took place in his premise.

Pastor Karabo: Did you claim with the insurance?

Tumelo: Yes, but I had to pay access of R8,000 ($1,000).

Pastor Karabo: Don't be discouraged. The Lord will bless you again.

Tumelo: It did not end there. While I was still dealing with the loss of my car, I had a strange call from one of my clients I supply with my herbal teas, who claimed that the tea did not taste the same, could not see good results from my product.

Pastor Karabo: And then?

Tumelo: I asked the client to return the products, and to my surprise, I discovered that our product has been faked.

Pastor Karabo: No, Tumelo!

Tumelo: I opened a case and did my own investigation and had a shock of my life when I discovered that my own PA (personal assistant) and her husband and our former driver have been faking my product and supplying my clients.

Pastor Karabo: Did you confront your PA?

Tumelo: I didn't have to. She gave me a letter of resignation even before I could suspect her or anyone. I hired a private investigator, who discovered that my PA and her partners in crime have been working with a big syndicate of herbal suppliers who were pushing and benefiting from the fake product. Furthermore, when they realized that there was an investigation, they went to all my clients claiming my product is a fake and is under investigation, and that affected our sales drastically, and users of my products become skeptical.

Pastor Karabo: People are ungrateful. You gave them jobs, but they were stealing from you.

Tumelo: These people where arrogant. They started panicking and using intimidation and threats to try and stop me from pursuing the case by sending people with guns to threaten my staff and also robbing and attacking my wife's stores, followed me with cars.

Pastor Karabo: Hectic stuff.

Tumelo: While dealing with this case, there was an attempt to steal one of my business cars by my own staff, but fortunately that evening, I was at home and heard some sound outside, called the armed response company, who helped me save that car.

Pastor Karabo: So God saved your other car.

Tumelo: I don't know about that. Why couldn't he save my Dodge?

Pastor Karabo: You are ungrateful, Tumelo.

Tumelo: Please, listen at all my stories then you will understand where I'm coming from.

Pastor Karabo: Still.

Tumelo: Let me proceed!

Pastor Karabo: OK.

Tumelo: Few weeks later, my factory was broken into, and I lost computers, furniture, etc. And I then put a security guard, but still there was a second attempt, and I lost more though the security guard saved most of the staff by shooting in the air to scare the criminals.

Pastor Karabo: At least the guard was not harmed, and he saved most of your staff.

Tumelo: He failed to save all my staff.

Pastor Karabo: Why are you so attached to material things?

Tumelo: I've worked hard for them.

Pastor Karabo: Even then, you know as a believer, they are from God, and surely he will bless you again and again.

Tumelo: So must I be happy when I lose them?

Pastor Karabo: You must be grateful you had them. You must be grateful you still have some.

Tumelo: I'm grateful of what I had and have!

Pastor Karabo: So why are you so angry at God? Why do you blame him when you know he will bless you again?

Tumelo: I live in fear, thinking he will take all that I have.

Pastor Karabo: What else have you lost?

Tumelo: We experienced a gross theft at our stores.

Pastor Karabo: You mean the nine stores that you and your wife have?

Tumelo: Correct!

Pastor Karabo: Surely you should still generate enough income to meet your expenses and business needs.

Tumelo: Actually we are left with only two stores now!

Pastor Karabo: What happened to your other seven stores?

Tumelo: As I said, we were hit by gross theft of our stock and money by our own staff. Worse, the recession hit us so badly that we found ourselves in so much debt that those stores were no longer generating enough income to sustain themselves.

Pastor Karabo: Didn't you have a control system for stock, money, etc?

Tumelo: Pastor, a research has shown that there are more than four hundred ways to steal. How many do you know? How many do I know?

Pastor Karabo: Continue.

Tumelo: As I speak to you, the remaining two stores are battling to pay the backlog of the debt caused by our nine stores, owing suppliers, credit cards, overdraft, retrenchment packages, tax, loans, leases, etc.

Pastor Karabo: Recession has hit everyone, not just you. At least you still have two stores. Other people's are closed completely.

Tumelo: So I'm ungrateful?

Pastor Karabo: You are too hard on yourself. You should count your blessings and thank the Lord.

Tumelo: At one stage I thought change is good. I need to invest in other things.

Pastor Karabo: So why don't you?

Tumelo: I did. I bought secondhand trucks to transport coal in the mines, and I found myself in more debt than before as I had six trucks. Now and then, the money generated went back into fixing trucks, paying diesel, dealing with mine strikes, waiting for weeks before the next stock pile is ready, etc.

Pastor Karabo: Tumelo, you had it rough. I understand your frustrations, anger, disappointments, but still, I don't understand why you blame God and not Satan or yourself for the decisions you made. But do not be discouraged. We both shall explore your situation and see who to blame, for what and whether, there is any way out of these situations.

Tumelo: I have even started having health issues. I know I've done lots of mistakes, but where is God who promised his children that he is forgiving, loving and answers our prayers and is gracious and merciful and that he will never leave us nor forsake us? You know, honestly I don't see myself surviving this year. I worry about my kids who are still young and my wife who still needs a companion.

Pastor Karabo: I have listened to you talk and remember Job's stories, and I relate to yours. We are going to explore his stories and others related from the Bible and compare them with yours and see if the god who helped his children yesterday, will he not do the same for you today? We start tomorrow. Bring your Bible and notebook. The real work starts! Good night for now.

Tumelo: Good night, Pastor.

Chapter 2

Man and His Decisions

Pastor Karabo: Morning, Tumelo, I hope you are ready and excited as I am to listen to what God has to say to us today. Would you like to pray?

Tumelo: Pastor, not that I mind, but honestly, I don't have the strength and the energy to pray, and I don't even know where to start, what to say.

Pastor Karabo: Let's close our eyes. Heavenly Father, we thank you for this opportunity and privilege to study your word and apply it to our current challenges. In Christ's name, our Lord. Amen.

Tumelo: Thank you!

Pastor Karabo: I have listened to your stories, sad as they may be, but with God nothing is impossible. You have been talking and I did most of the listening, but now, I need your undivided attention so that we both find solutions for your problems in the Word of God. Furthermore, my role is not to judge you, blame you, or criticize you but to firmly help you find and face the truth.

Tumelo: Am I allowed to question, disagree, and state my mind?"

Pastor Karabo: Of course. Remember, I don't hold the answers, but the Word of God does. Whatever statement we make, we must back it with the Word of God so that it is not from us but from his word.

Tumelo: I like that!

Pastor Karabo: We are going to look at you, Satan, and God in relation to your problems and motivate or justify with the Word of God who should take the blame for each individual's incident and why.

Tumelo: Who do we start with?

Pastor Karabo: You, I'm afraid.

Tumelo: All the better, I am sure there is very little you will find.

Pastor Karabo: Arrogance leads to misjudgment, my son! If you are honest with yourself, you will see, accept, realize how imperfect you are as a human being and how easy it is to pass the buck to or blame others when actually, to a great extent, you are the cause of your own misfortunes.

Tumelo: Shall we start?

Pastor Karabo: When we met the first night, you said you are devastated, destroyed, God has turned against you, and now you have no peace, quietness, rest but only turmoil, am I right?

Tumelo: True! I was quoting Job.

Pastor Karabo: You furthermore said, while swimming in wealth, it became difficult to serve God, study his word, put him first and, out of guilt, feared one day he will take

Cowards die many times before their death, but brave men die once.

(William Shakespeare)

What I fear has come upon me, what I dreaded has happened to me. Now I have no peace, no quietness, I have no rest, but only turmoil.

(Job 3:25-26)

When you have the Word of God in you, you have freedom from fear, worry, anxiety, hostility, pride, and jealousy, and guilt complex.

(Epigram)

your wealth! Correct?

Tumelo: Correct.

Pastor Karabo: Now because of your guilt, you have concluded that now God is making you pay as expected.

Tumelo: Is there any other explanation?

Pastor Karabo: Have you thought about, while you were drunk in a pool of wealth, you started making some of the wrong, careless, and foolish decisions, which God has nothing to do with?

Statistics are like a bikini! What they reveal is suggestive, what they hide is vital.

(Epigram)

We do not see things as they are, but we see things as we are.

(Epigram)

For the wrath of man will praise God.

(Ps. 76:10)

Tumelo: Such as what?

Pastor Karabo: Let's start with your stores. If you had a control system, how come it took you long to see that you were losing stock or money from your stores, or are you going to blame God for not being a security guard over your stock or money? Whose responsibility is it to look after things that God blesses us with? God? Or you? From your monthly report,

I have come to know how to get along with humble means, and I also know how to live in prosperity, in any and every circumstance. I have learned the secret of being filled and going hungry, both having abundance and suffering need.

(Phil 14:12)

Don't let your appearance cause you disappearance.

(Epigram)

Let no one say when he is tempted, I am being tempted from God, for God cannot be tempted from evil. Furthermore, he himself does not tempt anyone.

(James 1:13)

cash flow, day-end report, were you not able to see that you were losing money or stock, and if you knew very little about how the business runs, why didn't you do a basic course on financial control or management or ask for help? Yet you blame God for your ignorance and laziness.

Tumelo: I trust my staff.

Pastor Karabo: Tumelo, does being

Dreams do come true, provided you stay awake when you dream.

(Epigram)

Though success may be sweet but it has a smell of sweat.

(Epigram)

But I hold this against you; you have abandoned your most important love, the Lord Jesus Christ.

(Rev 2:4)

a Christian mean you stop using your common sense?

Tumelo: I thought I had a good team.

Pastor Karabo: How is it God's fault that you where losing so much stock and money? Who was negligent? God or you?

Tumelo: Maybe it's me.

Pastor Karabo: Maybe, Tumelo?

Tumelo: I get your point, Pastor.

Pastor Karabo: No, I don't think

You change your thoughts, you change your world.

(Epigram)

Ignorance does not mean you don't know, it means you don't care.

(Epigram)

Happiness to the man who finds wisdom and the man who gains understanding.

(Prov 3; 13)

you do. You see yourself as a victim in this situation and that it cannot be you, and I am surprised that you are not blaming Satan as well.

Tumelo: I do blame him too for bringing these misfortunes and making life difficult for us.

Pastor Karabo: What about you, Tumelo, what about your decisions and the choice you made?

Tumelo: I try to do well. I care for others, I am considerate, I give, I pray, I fast, I don't

Do not fear for I am with you; do not anxiously look about you, for I am your God. I will strengthen you, surely I will help you, and surely I will uphold you with my righteous right hand.

(Isa. 41:10)

Fear does not exist in love, but mature love drives out this fear, for this fear causes punishment. In fact, he who is afraid has not been matured in love.

(1 John 4:18)

But Moses said to the people "Do not fear! Stand by and see the deliverance of the Lord, which he will accomplish for you today".

(Ex. 14; 13)

steal, I help those who are sick, I love my family, friends, relatives, and neighbors.

Pastor Karabo: You are deviating as usual, avoiding the real question. What about you, Tumelo, are you not accountable or responsible for the decisions you make or its consequences? You talk about your good work. I'm talking about your decisions, who is responsible and accountable for them. Later we will explore your good

By this love of God has been manifested in our case, because God has sent his unique Son into the world in order that we might live by means of him.

(1 John 4: 9)

If you are going to climb a tree, you are going to have to grab the branches and not the blossom.

(Epigram)

Knowledge puff up, but love edifies.

(1 Cor 8; 1)

works, but for now we focus on your decisions, right?

Tumelo: Right!

Pastor Karabo: Let's go back to when your factory was broken into. Don't you have an alarm system or cameras?

Tumelo: Yes, an alarm system which works on and off!

Pastor Karabo: So your alarm system was not working properly?

Tumelo: Yes.

Pastor Karabo: And you knew that?

For this fear causes punishment.

(1 John 4:18)

"Fear is false evidence appearing real.

(Epigram)

"Fear does not exist where there is love.

(1 John 4; 18)

Tumelo: I guess.

Pastor Karabo: And you did nothing about it.

Tumelo: I never thought they will break in.

Pastor Karabo: If that's the case, why did you put it in the first place?

Tumelo: To provide security.

Pastor Karabo: How?

Tumelo: Pastor, I know I made a mistake. I should have been more responsible.

Pastor Karabo: You made a foolish

If therefore the light that is in you is darkness, how great is the darkness!

(Matt. 6: 23)

For I say, through the grace which has been given to me, to everyone who is among you, stop thinking of self in terms of arrogance beyond what you ought to think in terms of sanity for the purpose of being rational without illusion, as God has assigned to each one a standard from doctrine.

(Rom. 12:3)

For I am convinced that neither death nor life, nor angels, nor principalities, nor things present, nor things to come, nor power, nor height, nor depth, nor any other created thing shall separate us from the love of God, which is in Christ Jesus our Lord. (Rom. 8:38-39)

mistake, moron, and you have a nerve to blame God and Satan for your mess.

Tumelo: I should have been more careful.

Pastor Karabo: You later tightened your security by putting a guard, which was a great idea. There was a second attempt where your guard managed to safeguard some of your assets, and instead of celebrating what was saved, you ignore that and focus

Be not descended, evil companion's_corrupt good morals.

(1 Cor. 15:33)

Ignorance does not mean you don't know. It means you don't care.

(Epigram)

Make it your ambition to lead a quite life, mind your own business so that you are not depended on anyone nor live under anyone's shadow.

(1 Thess. 4:11)

on what you lost and blame God and Satan for it. Are you aware that maybe if you fixed the alarm after the first robbery and also adding a guard that could have saved all your belongings?

Tumelo: Possibly.

Pastor Karabo: Did you thank God for all the assets which were saved?

Tumelo: I don't remember!

And make straight paths for your feet, lest that which is lame be turned out of the way, but let it rather be healed.

(Heb 12:13)

Therefore, brethren, everything that is true, and everything that is honourable, everything that is righteous, everything that is pure, everything that is capacity for love, everything that is commendable, if there is any virtue and anything worthy of praise, concentrate on these things.

(Phil 4:8)

He who walks with wise men will be wise, but the companion of fools will suffer evil.

(Prov. 13:20)

Pastor Karabo: I'm not surprised you probably did not!

Tumelo: I was too angry, bitter, and tired from these constant misfortunes!

Pastor Karabo: Angry at whom? Ooh! Let me guess, at God! Right?

Tumelo: Right!

Pastor Karabo: How predictable.

Tumelo: Am I bad?

Pastor Karabo: You are real, you are human!

The size of a man is measured by the size of things that make him angry.

(Epigram)

Bitterness is like faeces and urine you throw to other people. It leads to hatred, revenge, jealousy, envy, and malice.

(Epigram)

And be not conformed to this world, but be ye transformed by the renewing of your mind, that ye may prove what is that good and acceptable, and perfect, will of God.

(Rom 12:2)

Tumelo: These problems have drained me. I have no energy, no excitement anymore. Every day I wake up, I wonder what's coming my way, but I know trouble is certain.

Pastor Karabo: And you don't realize that grace is also guaranteed.

Tumelo: Certainly not to me!

Pastor Karabo: You are naive and stubborn.

Tumelo: I am real, as you said.

In everything give thanks, for this is the will of God in Christ Jesus concerning you.

(1 Thess. 5:18)

In order to win greater battles you have to win first battles of pettiness.

(Epigram)

For by grace are ye saved through faith, and that not of yourselves, it is the gift of God, not of works, lest any man should boast.

(Eph. 2:8-9)

Pastor Karabo: I don't understand. If you had so much wealth, how did you end up owing suppliers, credit cards, overdraft, retrenchment packages, loans, and leases? Why didn't you use cash and be free of debts?

Tumelo: I did not want to use my own money. Wealthy people never use their own money but somebody else's money to generate their own.

For the joy of the Lord is your strength.

(Neh. 8:10)

Suffering does not always come to injure, but provide more opportunities to remind us of the present of God.

(Epigram)

He that is greedy of gain troubleth his own house, but he that hateth gifts shall live.

(Prov. 15:27)

Pastor Karabo: Greed is not good!

Tumelo: It wasn't greed!

Pastor Karabo: What was it? God again? Against you?

Tumelo: It was recession!

Pastor Karabo: Not bad planning?

Tumelo: I made good investments.

Pastor Karabo: Then why are you in trouble? My basic accounting may not be good, but were you not supposed to pay your expenses and liabilities and use your profit to increase

And he said unto him, take head and beware of covetousness; for a man's life consisteth not in the abundance of the things which he possesseth.

(Luke 12: 15)

If anyone teaches a different doctrine and does not concur with sound doctrine, namely those doctrines of our Lord Jesus Christ, even to that doctrine pertaining to Godliness, he has received arrogance, understanding nothing.

(1 Tim. 6:3-4)

For bombastically speaking arrogant words from the source of emptiness, they keep enticing by lusts, by lasciviousness, those who barely escape from those who live in error.

(2 Pet. 2:18)

your assets base so that you increase your profit margins?

Tumelo: I tried all that, but my asset base (the nine stores) stopped generating income to pay liabilities and expenses and generating profit to increase my asset base, hence I am left with such a huge backlog of debts.

Pastor Karabo: So God has sabotaged you and put you into debts?

Tumelo: "I think so. I think

If we confess our sins, He is faithful and righteous with the result that he forgives us our sins and also cleanses us from all unrighteousness.

(1 John 1: 9)

Be of sober spirit, be on the alert. Your adversary, the devil, prowls about like a roaring lion, seeking someone to devour. But resist him, firm in your faith.

(1 Pet. 5:8-9)

He made him, who knew no sin to be sin on our behalf that we might become the righteousness of God in him.

(2 Cor. 5:21)

I am paying the price of ignoring him.

Pastor Karabo: So you don't take the responsibility or accountability for your fall.

Tumelo: Not entirely! Pastor, I have tried everything to change my situation.

Pastor Karabo: Like what? Investing in trucks that were not in good condition?"

Tumelo: At least I tried!

Pastor Karabo: Tumelo, did you check

Testing has not caught up with you except the human kind, moreover, God is faithful, who will not permit you to be tested beyond your capabilities, but with the testing he will also provide a way out so that you can endure it.

(1 Cor. 10:13)

Wear for yourselves the full armour from God that you may be able to hold your ground against the tactics of the devil

(Eph. 6:11)

For this reason, many among you are weak and sick, and a number sleep. But if we judged ourselves rightly, we should not be judged.

(2 Cor. 11:30-31)

the service book of those, trucks before you bought them? Did you check the mileage of those trucks? Did you research about the coal or mine business before investing in it? Did you ask yourself why the former owner of those trucks would sell them if they were generating income for him?

Tumelo: Not really.

Pastor Karabo: And yet God

Who can understand his errors cleanse thou me from secret faults.

(Ps. 19:12)

One thing have I desired of the Lord, that will I seek after, that I may dwell in the house of the Lord, and to enquire in his temple.

(Ps. 27:4)

Come to me, all who are weary and heavy laden, and I will give you rest, take my yoke upon you, and learn from me, for I am gentle and humble in heart, and you shall find rest for your souls. For my yoke is easy and my load is light.

(Matt. 11:28-30)

becomes the scapegoat!

Tumelo: I prayed for guidance before I bought them.

Pastor Karabo: Therefore, that justifies your ignorance, laziness, and foolishness of impulsive investments.

Tumelo: I realize my mistakes, but I tried a lot of things to regain God's forgiveness and reconciliations.

Pastor Karabo: What things?

Tumelo: Praying in tongues, giving, fasting,

A wise man will hear, and will increase learning and a man of understanding shall attain unto wise counsels.

(Prov. 1:5)

Awake to righteousness, and sin not for some have not the knowledge of God, I speak this to your shame.

(1 Cor. 15:34)

But there is forgiveness with thee, that thou mayest be feared.

(Ps. 130:4)

consulting spiritualists for advice, ancestors, going to church, witnessing, etc.

Pastor Karabo: So you think these things should take away or wipe your wrong decisions?

Tumelo: How else can I remove this spell?

Pastor Karabo: I'm glad you ask that question. This makes me realize that now you are ready to learn and face the fact, and ready to account, so

For all the gods of the people are idols, but the Lord made the heavens.

(1 Chron. 16:26)

Call upon me in the day of trouble, I will deliver thee, and thou shall glorify me.

(Ps. 50:15)

Do not look where you fell, but where you slipped.

(African proverb)

Some people are ready to learn but they are not willing to be tough.

(Epigram)

tomorrow, we get into real business. Before you leave, can I offer you coffee?

Tumelo: I would love that.

Pastor Karabo: Remember the basic requirement: I'm the teacher, you are the student. The Bible is your textbook, and my office is your classroom.

Tumelo: Thanks for the coffee, and see you tomorrow.

The word of God is quick and powerful, and sharper than any two edged sword, piercing even to the dividing asunder of soul and spirit, and of joints and marrow, and is a discerner of the thoughts and intents of the heart.

(Heb. 4:12)

All scripture is given by inspiration of God, and is profitable for doctrine, for reproof, for correction, for instruction in righteousness, that the man of God may be perfect, thoroughly furnished unto all good works.

(2 Tim. 3:16-17)

Study to show thyself approved unto God, a workman that need not to be ashamed, rightly dividing the word of truth.

(2 Tim. 2:15)

Pastor Karabo: Good morning, Tumelo!

Tumelo: Morning, Pastor.

Pastor Karabo: I realize you are coughing this morning.

Tumelo: A small flu.

Pastor Karabo: I'm going to make a good mixture which will help: garlic, lemon, ginger, and honey in a cup of boiled water.

Tumelo: Great!

Pastor Karabo: We pray, as usual. Heavenly Father, thank you for this opportunity to study you word. May God the holy spirit

Seek ye first the kingdom of God, and all these things will be added unto you.

(Matt. 6:33)

Call unto me and I will answer thee and show thee great and mighty things, which thou know not.

(Jer. 33:3)

No one has fellowship with God who keeps advancing out of bounds and does not remain through the doctrine of Christ.

2 John 9

lead and teach us as we seek answers from your word. Amen.

Tumelo: Amen.

Pastor Karabo: It's a good thing that you care for others, are considerate, giving, pray, do not steal, help the sick, and love your family, friends, and neighbors, seek advice, go to church, and witness. But is the reason for doing all these great things motivated by the fact that you are

A small gift will do if your heart is big enough.

(Epigram)

But all these worketh that one and the self same spirit, dividing to every man severally as he will.

(1 Cor. 12:11)

But that same spirit explicitly communicates that in later periods of time some will fall away from doctrine, paying attention to deceitful spirits and concentrating on doctrines of demons.

(1 Tim. 4:1)

trying to stop your misfortunes or to retain your wealth and comfortable lifestyle?

Tumelo: Yes, but also to please God!

Pastor Karabo: My son, there only thing that can please God is faith in him!

Tumelo: Faith alone?

Pastor Karabo: Faith alone! And not your good works.

Tumelo: Then what's the point?

Pastor Karabo: Firstly, let's explore

God blesses you because of his righteousness and not because of your good works.

(Epigram)

Knowing that a man is not justified by the work of the law, but by the faith of Jesus Christ.

(Gal. 2:16)

For by grace are ye saved through faith, and that not of yourselves; it is the gift of God; not of works.

(Eph. 42:8)

your good works, and then we will address your question about what's the point.

Tumelo: I thought the good we do is equally important.

Pastor Karabo: The good you do is great, but the motive behind it is even more important!

Tumelo: What motive?

Pastor Karabo: You just told me that you do good to change your misfortune and also to please God, right?

Neurotic person—builds a castle in the air.

(Epigram)

Psychotic person lives in that castle.

(Epigram)

Psychiatrist collects the rent for that castle.

(Epigram)

Tumelo: Right!

Pastor Karabo: And I am saying, your good works and the motive behind it are what God looks at, and furthermore, you said you want to please God, and I'm saying only faith can please God and not your good work.

Tumelo: You are not making sense!

Pastor Karabo: Then let's look at just two of your good works to illustrate my point.

Tumelo: OK!

This is the only thing I want to find out from you, did you receive the spirit by the works of the law, or by hearing with faith? Are you so foolish? Having begun by the spirit, are you now being perfected by the flesh.

(Gal. 3:2-3)

For without faith, it is impossible to please God.

(Heb. 11:6)

For you are all sons of God through faith in Christ Jesus. For all of you who were baptized into Christ have clothed yourselves with Christ.

(Gal. 3:26-27)

Pastor Karabo: Giving is a wonderful thing, but to give because you want your misfortunes to be stopped or your wealth, health to be returned is rather manipulative. So you give to bribe God to stop your misfortunes, return your good health and wealth, is that not selfish or arrogant? Tumelo, the right thing must be done the right way.

Tumelo: The right way?

Pastor Karabo: Yes, the right way! The wrong thing done the wrong way is obviously wrong, but the right

Every man according as he purpose in his heart, so let him give; not grudgingly or of necessity; for God love that cheerful giver.

(2 Cor. 9:7)

You can give compassion.

(Epigram)

Quality is much more than quantity.

(Epigram)

thing done the wrong way is also wrong. God loves a cheerful giver and not a giver who wants a return on his investment. Giving does not mean much, it means everything.

Tumelo: But surely you should be blessed for giving.

Pastor Karabo: God blesses you because of who he is and not because of your filthy good works. God blesses you because of his love for you, his grace and mercy upon you, and you don't earn it nor deserve it.

For in Jesus Christ neither circumcision awaileth_any thing, nor uncircumcision; but faith which worketh by love.

(Gal. 5:6)

The greatest disaster that can befall a person is to have eyes and fail to see.

(Epigram)

For by grace are ye saved through faith; that not of yourselves; it is the gift of God; not of works, lest any man should boast?

Eph 2; 8-9

Tumelo: So what about 10 percent to the church?

Pastor Karabo: What about it?

Tumelo: Won't God bless you for paying 10 percent of your salary of business to the church?

Pastor Karabo: Rubbish!

Tumelo: Oops!

Pastor Karabo: In the olden days 10 percent was paid by both believers and unbelievers as a form of tax to run the country since

Now concerning the collection for the saints, as I have given order to the churches of Galatia, even so do ye. Upon the first day of the week let every one of you lay by him in store as God hath prospered him, that there be no gatherings when I come.

(1 Cor. 16:1-2)

Blessed is he that expects nothing, for he shall never be disappointed.

(Epigram)

Therefore, if any man is in Christ he is a new creature, the old things passed way, behold, new things have come.

2 Cor 5; 17

in those days the country was run by the church. But today, freewill offering is what the church needs to run the administration, expenses, missionary work of the church to reach out to the communities by promoting the gospel free of charge so that no person is disadvantaged to hear or get the opportunity to have access to the Word of God. Ten percent is not a tool created

For if there be first a willing mind, it is accepted according to that a man hath, and not according to that he hath not.

(2 Cor. 8:12)

Ignorance becomes cognisance if you study the word of God, uncertainty becomes confidence, potential becomes hope.

(Epigram)

Set your mind on the things above, not on the things that are on earth.

(Col. 3:2)

to enrich the pastors and their deacon friends, and whether you pay 10 or 20 or 50 percent of your profit income to church is of irrelevance. The motive behind giving should be right, and the use for that gift to the church should be for the glorification of Christ and not you or me.

Tumelo: So I don't have to give 10 percent to the church?"

Pastor Karabo: You can give nothing if you

The amount you give is not important but the motive behind giving.

(Epigram)

Even the hypocrites admire righteousness that's why they imitate it.

(Epigram)

Every man according as he purposeth in his heart, so let him give, not grudgingly, or of necessity; for God loveth a cheerful giver.

(2 Cor. 9:7)

do not have. You can give 1 percent, 2 percent, 20 percent, 30 percent, etc. It is the motive behind giving, for the ministry of God to grow and not for return on your investment. Whatever God has blessed you with, he did so because of his grace, mercy, and love for you. You do not deserve anything from God. It is pure grace, you can't earn it, and so is salvation.

You can never lose, when you do things God's way.

(Epigram)

And all this assembly shall know that the Lord saveth not with sword and spear, for the battle is the Lord's, and he will give you into our hands.

(1 Sam. 17:47)

And if I have the gift of prophecy and know all mysteries and all knowledge, and if I have all faith, so as to remove mountains but do not have love, I am nothing.

1 Cor. 13:2

Tumelo: So I just pray to God to remove my misfortunes.

Pastor Karabo: Yes, you do!

Tumelo: But I have. He is not responding.

Pastor Karabo: What makes you think he is not responding?

Tumelo: I'm still in trouble, and my situation worsens every day.

Pastor Karabo: God always answers our prayers. Maybe he is not answering in your way or as you desire, and if he decides not to answer

And all things, whatever use shall ask in prayer, believing, ye shall receive.

(Matt. 21:22)

Therefore I say unto you, what things so ever ye desire, when ye pray, believe that ye receive them, and ye shall have them.

(Mark 11:24)

And it shall come to pass, that before they call, I will answer, and while they are yet speaking, I will hear.

Isa. 65:24

there may be reasons.

Tumelo: Reasons?

Pastor Karabo: Yes, reasons!

Tumelo: What reasons?

Pastor Karabo: Firstly, let's look at why we pray. Secondly, look at how do we pray, and lastly address your question: what reasons would hinder your prayer?

Tumelo: Can I have that mixture you made for me this morning? It stopped my cough.

Pastor Karabo: All you do is put a teaspoon of garlic, slice of lemon, and a teaspoon

Ye lust, and have not; ye kill, and desire to have, and cannot obtain: ye fight and war, yet ye have not, because ye ask not, ye ask, and receive not, because ye ask amiss, that ye may consume it upon your lusts.

(James 4:2-3)

Whose stoppeth his ears at the cry of poor, he also shall cry himself, but shall not be heard.

(Prov. 21:13)

But if they obey not, they shall perish by the sword, and they shall die without knowledge.

Job 35; 12-13

of honey. Why don't you do it yourself so that you learn?

Tumelo: Can I make one for you too?

Pastor Karabo: Yes, I would love some.

Tumelo: You know, Pastor, I have tried every prayer, tongues, kneeling, meditation, fasting and praying, candles, oils, etc.

Pastor Karabo: Praying in tongues?

Tumelo: Yes, Pastor, don't you pray in tongues?

Pastor Karabo: What is that, Tumelo?

And this is the confidence that we have in him, that, if we ask any thing according to his will, he heareth us.

(1 John 5:14)

And what so ever we ask, we receive of him, because we keep his commandments, and do those things that are pleasing in his sight.

(1 John 3:22)

Again I say unto you, that if two of you shall agree on earth agree about anything that they shall ask, it shall be done for them of my father which is in heaven.

Matt 18; 19

Tumelo: Are you being sarcastic?

Pastor Karabo: Do you pray in tongues?

Tumelo: Don't you, Pastor?

Pastor Karabo: Tumelo, this is serious stuff. I am going to close my eyes, and you are going to pray in tongues, starting now!

Tumelo: Really?

Pastor Karabo: Really!

Tumelo: *Ra baba raba raba, kabla kish, kabla kushu, rababa, rondo, majaran, borotha.*

Pastor Karabo: Is this your mother tongue?

Love never fails, but if there are gifts of prophecy, they will be done away, if there are tongues, the will cease.

(1 Cor. 13:8)

If anyone speaks in tongue, it should be by two or at the most three, and each in turn, and let one interpret, but if there is no interpreter, let him keep silent in the church and let him speak to himself and to God.

(1 Cor. 14:27-28)

If I speak with the tongues of men and of angels, but do not have love, I have become a noisy gong or a changing cymbal.

(1 Cor. 13:1)

Tumelo: No! It's not my mother tongue!

Pastor Karabo: What is your mother tongue?

Tumelo: Sotho.

Pastor Karabo: Were you praying in sotho?

Tumelo: No.

Pastor Karabo: Why do you speak sotho?

Tumelo: To communicate with my family, friends, community, and God.

Pastor Karabo: So you agree that you speak sotho to make sense to everyone who speaks and

So also you, since you are zealous of spiritual gift, seek to abound for the edification of the church.

(1 Cor. 14:12)

Yet even lifeless things, either flute or harp, in producing a sound, if they do not produce a distinction in the tones, how will it be known what is played on the flute or harp.

(1 Cor. 14:7)

Emotionalism misleads and obscures the truth of bible doctrine.

(Epigram)

understands your language?

Tumelo: Correct!

Pastor Karabo: Now when you prayed just now, you were communicating with God, right?

Tumelo: Right.

Pastor Karabo: Just out of curiosity, what were you saying to God?

Tumelo: What do you mean?

Pastor Karabo: What were you communicating with God?

Tumelo: I don't know, but he understands!

Call unto me, and I will answer thee, and show thee great and mighty things, which thou knowest not.

(Jer. 33:3)

But let all things be done properly and in an orderly manner.

(1 Cor. 14:40)

In the law it is written, by men of strong tongue and by the lips of strangers, I will speak to this people and even so they will not listen to me says the Lord. So then tongues are for a sign not to those who believe but to unbelievers.

(1 Cor. 14:21-22)

Pastor Karabo: Then if he understands and you don't, then what was the purpose of your tongues?

Tumelo: To confuse Satan.

Pastor Karabo: To confuse Satan or yourself?

Tumelo: This is confusing.

Pastor Karabo: You have been confusing yourself with the garbage you are fed by religion.

Tumelo: Then what is the purpose of tongues?

Pastor Karabo: Rather you ask, what was the purpose of tongues?

So also you, unless you utter by the tongue speech that is clear, how will it be known what is spoken? For you will be speaking into the air.

(1 Cor. 14:9)

Guard what been entrusted to you avoiding worldly and empty chatter.

(1 Tim. 6:20)

This is the only thing I want find out from you, did you receive the spirit by the works of the law, or by hearing with faith? Are you so foolish? Having begun by the spirit, are you now being perfect by the flesh.

Gal 3; 2-3

Tumelo: Are you saying we no longer speak in tongues?

Pastor Karabo: Though Paul made it clear that tongues will cease, but if it still exists? Is it for confusing Satan?

Tumelo: Complex subject!

Pastor Karabo: Nothing is complex. The problem is we quote or misuse the Word of God out of context for our own selfish desires.

Tumelo: What could be selfish about tongues?

But when the perfect comes, the partial will be done away.

(1 Cor. 13:10)

If therefore the whole church should assemble together and all speak in tongues, and ungifted men or unbelievers enter, will they not say that you are mad?

(1 Cor. 14:23)

Be not deceived, evil communications corrupt good manners.

(1 Cor 15; 33)

Pastor Karabo: Tumelo, tongues today are being used to gain power, membership, and control over people who are vulnerable, who are in pain, who need help from the church, who need most importantly the gospel and doctrine in their soul to help them deal and understand the challenges in their lives and not pseudo or hypocritical activities such as giving, praying in tongues, healing, and prophecy!

Tumelo: So the tongues are not real?

Guard what been entrusted to you avoiding worldly and empty chatter.

(1 Tim. 6:20)

For if I pray in a tongue, my spirit prays, but my mind is unfruitful. What is the outcome then? I shall pray with the spirit and I shall pray with the mind also, I shall sing with the spirit and I shall sing with mind also.

(1 Cor. 14:14-15)

When I was a child, I use to speak as a child, think as a child, reason as a child, when i became a man; I did away with childish things.

(1 Cor. 13:11)

Pastor Karabo: If you pray in tongues, there needs to be an interpreter for edification of the church.

Tumelo: I don't know what to say.

Pastor Karabo: The gibberish rhyming sounds you were making sounded more like emotions or self-entertainment, not tongues.

Tumelo: What are you saying to me, Pastor?

Pastor Karabo: Listen to me, my boy! Tongues were used by God the Holy Spirit through the disciples, preachers to edify people

Being emotional does not make you a better or worse person.

(Epigram)

Emotions is nothing but self-entertainment.

(Epigram)

However, in the church I desire to speak five words with my mind, that I may instruct others also, rather than ten thousand words in a tongue.

(1 Cor. 14:19)

and not a language to confuse Satan, so as to uplift or encourage spiritual improvement or growth in knowledge even for those who could not read or understand the language used then.

Tumelo: Yes!

Pastor Karabo: Yes! Tongues are or were for strengthening fellowship with God and spiritual growth of believers and unbelievers to come to know Christ

But the spirit explicitly says that in later times, some will fall away from the faith, paying attention to deceitful spirit and doctrines of demons.

1 Tim. 4:1

God makes sense and communicates with us in a manner that makes sense.

Epigram

Now I wish that you all spoke in tongues, but even more that you would prophesy, and greater is one who prophesies than one who speaks in tongues, unless he interprets, so that the church may receive edifying.

1 Cor. 14:5

and encouragement of positive attitude toward the word of God. Today the scriptures are translated into every language, and therefore God today speaks or communicate with us through his word only, in our own mother tongues! God no longer talks to us through disciples, prophets, dreams, visions, but through his word (the Bible) only.

All scripture is God—breathed, and is profitable for doctrine, for reproof, for correction, for instruction in righteousness that the man of God might be mature, thoroughly furnished unto all good works.

2 Tim. 3:16-17

The Bible is the plan of God the father, the mind of Christ and the voice of God the Holy Spirit.

Epigram

For I am convinced that neither death, nor life, nor angels, nor principalities, nor things present, nor things to come, nor power, nor height, nor depth, nor any other created thing, shall separate us from the love of God, which is in Christ Jesus our Lord

Rom. 8:38-39

So you see, your misfortunes cannot be fixed by your so-called praying in tongues.

Tumelo: I am embarrassed.

Pastor Karabo: You are learning. You are growing.

Tumelo: Interesting!

Pastor Karabo: Now that we have addressed the tongue saga, let focus on how do we pray!

Tumelo: Firstly, what is prayer?

That whatever you might ask of the Father in the name, He may give to you.

John 15:16

And he said unto me, my grace is sufficient. For thee, for my strength is made perfect in weakness. Most gladly therefore will I rather glory in my infirmities that the power of Christ may rest upon me.

2 Cor. 12:9

And when this sound occurred, the multitude came together, and were believed because they were each one hearing them speak in his own language, and they were amazed marvelled, saying; why are not all these who are speaking Galileans? And how is it that we each hear them in our own language to which we were born?

Acts 2:6-8

Pastor Karabo: "It's communication between man and God, the only way today which we make a request to God."

Tumelo: "The only way?"

Pastor Karabo: Yes. In this church age, God communicates with us through his word (the Bible), and we communicate with him through prayer alone. No more messengers, no more dreams, no more visions, etc. The Word of God is complete and has all the answers to your problems and guidance.

Man shall not live on bread alone but on every word that proceeds out of the mouth of God.

Matt. 4:4

The word of God is alive and powerful, sharper than any two-edged sword, piercing even to the dividing asunder of the soul and the spirit, and of the joints and the marrow, and is a critic of thoughts and intents of the heart.

Heb. 4:12

Call unto me, and I will answer thee, and show the great and mighty things, which thou knowest not.

Jer 33; 3

Tumelo: Then why does he not answer my prayer?

Pastor Karabo: God may not answer for few reasons such as praying with wrong motive, lack of faith, disobedience, not complying with God's will, pride, dishonoring your wife, no compassion for the poor, selfish motive, etc. If you lack faith, God will not hear you pray. Of all the things God hates is a proud look. If you do not honor your wife, you hinder your prayers. If you don't feel for

And what so ever we ask, we receive of him, because we keep his commandments, and do those things that are pleasing in his sight.

1 John 3:22

And this is the confidence that we have in him, that, if we ask any thing according to his will, he heareth us.

1 John 5:14

"There they cry, but none giveth answer, because of the pride of evil men. Surely God will not hear vanity, neither will he regard it"

Job 35;12-13

the poor, God will not hear your prayers. Your selfish motives have no place in God's presence, etc.

Tumelo: I never knew all this stuff.

Pastor Karabo: Furthermore, when you pray, you must confess your sins privately to God, give thanks for everything, pray for others and yourself.

Tumelo: I feel bad because all I do is to pray for myself, I hardly thank God for my blessing and

Ye lust, and have not, ye kill, and desire to have, and cannot obtain, ye fight and war, yet ye have not, because ye ask not. Ye ask and receive not because ye ask amiss, that ye may consume it upon your lusts.

(James 13:2-3)

Pray without ceasing.

(1 Thess. 5:17)

In everything give thanks, for this is the will of God in Christ Jesus concerning you.

(1 Thess. 5:18)

only confess my known sins sometimes. I realize that I have a hand to my miseries.

Pastor Karabo: Then we are getting somewhere, and to conclude this subject of prayer, you need to be aware that God answers your prayer according to his will. Sometimes he answers exactly the way you desire, but sometimes according to his own desire or plan for you.

Praying always with all prayer and supplication in the spirit, and watching thereunto with all perseverance and supplication for all saints.

(Eph 6:18)

And he gave them their request, but sent leanness into their soul.

(Psa. 106:15)

And call ye on the name of your gods, and I will call on the name of the Lord, and the God that answereth by fire, let him be God. And all the people answered and said, it is well spoken.

(1 Kings 18:24)

Tumelo: I know where to start now

Pastor Karabo: Where?

Tumelo: With prayer!

Pastor Karabo: Yes, Tumelo, now you are excited and motivated to recover from your situation, but before you pray for your misfortunes, you need to acknowledge your mistakes, foolish decisions, take accountability and responsibility for your mess instead of passing the buck to Satan or God. Maybe as part of your prayer

Thine own wickedness shall correct thee, and thy backslidings shall reprove thee, know therefore and see that it is an evil thing and bitter, that thou hast forsaken the Lord thy God, and that my fear is not in thee, saith the Lord God of hosts

Jer 2; 19

Return, ye backsliding children, and I will heal your backslidings. Behold, we come unto thee, for thou art the Lord our God.

(Jer. 3:22)

Thou hast forsaken me, saith the Lord, thou art gone backward, therefore will i stretch out my hand against thee, and destroy thee, I am weary with repenting.

(Jer. 15:6)

tell God about all the mess you created as you confess your sins for backsliding or being out of fellowship as a result of the decisions you made.

Tumelo: I get it, Pastor!

Pastor Karabo: I know some of the things that happened to you were not entirely caused by you, but you can't deny that you had a hand for most of your misfortunes.

Neither shall they defile themselves any more with their idols, nor with their detestable things, nor with any of their transgressions, but I will save them out of all their dwelling—place, where they have sinned, and will cleanse them, so shall they be my people, and I will be their God.

(Ezek. 37:23)

Ye are the sons of God by faith in Christ Jesus.

(Gal. 3:26)

And he himself bore our sins in his body on the cross.

(1 Pet. 2:24)

Tumelo: The more I think about it, the more I become angry at myself. I messed up big time.

Pastor Karabo: My son, you are not the first person to make mistakes. Most believers think once they become believers they become immune to nature taking its course.

Tumelo: Meaning?

Pastor Karabo: Whether you are a believer or not, if you make a wrong decision

For that which i do, I allow not, for what I would, that do I not, but what I hate, that do I.

(Rom. 7:15)

And he himself bore our sins in his body on the cross, that we might die to sin and live to righteousness, for by his wounds you were healed.

(1 Pet. 2:24)

He saved us, not on the basis of deeds which we have done in righteousness but according to his mercy, by the washing of regeneration and renewing by the Holy Spirit

Titus 3; 5

you will suffer the consequences. Garbage in, garbage out. You do not lose common sense now that you are a believer. You do not become immune to daily problems or challenges of life, but the difference is that as a believer in Christ you face the same problems that unbelievers face with God by your side. You have to remember that this is the devil's world and we are not yet in

For they sow the wind and they reap the whirlwind.

(Hos. 8:7)

He who sows iniquity will reap vanity.

(Prov. 22:8)

Do not be deceived, God is not mocked, for whatever a man sows this he will also reap.

Gal 6; 7

heaven, where there is peace and harmony.

Tumelo: Am I responsible for everything?

Pastor Karabo: You are also responsible for your mental sins such as jealousy, pride, envy, bitterness, anger, your verbal sins such as gossip, malign, judgment and physical sins such as murder, stealing, etc. I can go on and on with my list.

Tumelo: I realize that I have to account and take responsibility

For my thoughts are not your thoughts, neither are your ways my ways, saith the Lord.

(Isa. 55:8)

For as the heavens are higher than the earth, so are my ways higher than your ways, and my thoughts than your thoughts.

(Isa. 55:9)

Let the wicked forsake his way, and the unrighteous man his thoughts, and let him return unto the Lord, and he will have mercy upon him, and to our God, for he will abundantly pardon.

(Isa. 55:7)

for my mess, but, Pastor, are you saying Satan and God had no hand in my problems?

Pastor Karabo: I'm saying take responsibility for where you messed up and then we look at what role could Satan have played in your misfortunes and what has God allowed in the whole situation. Tomorrow we look at Satan and his role in your misfortunes.

Be transformed by the renewing of your mind.

(Rom. 12:2)

Our inner man is being renewed day by day.

(2 Cor. 4:16)

Be renewed in the spirit of your mind.

(Eph. 4:23)

Tumelo: I realize how much I've messed up. I have done lots of mistakes. I know I could have done things differently. I know I could have done things better. I know I should have confessed my sins of backsliding to my God. I know I should have admitted that I'm off the rail

And i am no more worthy to be called thy son, make me as one of thy hired servants.

(Luke 15:19)

And the son said unto him, Father, I have sinned against heaven, and in thy sight, and am no more worthy to be called thy son.

(Luke 15:21)

For this my son was dead and is alive again, he was lost and is found, and they began to be merry.

(Luke 15:24)

Instead of taking responsibility and accountability, I resorted to other things to try resolve my constant misfortunes.

Pastor Karabo: Yes, foolish things!

Tumelo: Pastor, I've tried everything possible: going to the cemetery with hope that my deceased parents have the power to change my misfortunes, being to the spiritual doctors to try a make sense why am I having so

For this purpose the son of God was manifest, that he might destroy the works of the devil.

(John 3:8)

Finally, my brethren, be strong in the Lord, and in the power of his might. Put on the whole armour of God that ye may be able to stand against the wiles of the devil.

(Eph. 6; 10-11)

But if I cast out devils by the spirit of God, then the kingdom of God is come unto you.

(Matt. 12:28)

much problems. Why am I losing everything? Washing with chicken's blood as suggested by the spiritualist to remove these spells, putting candles of all colors on every corner of my property, and calling on my ancestors and God to intervene, asking pastor friends to pray in my property hoping it will turn the tables, started going to

And when they shall say unto you seek unto them that have familiar spirits, and unto wizards that peep, and that mutter, should not a people seek unto their God for the living to the dead.

(Isa. 8:19)

For from within, out of the heart of men, proceed evil thoughts, adulteries, fornications, murderers, theft, covetousness, wickedness, deceit, lasciviousness an evil eye, blasphemy, pride, foolishness, all these evil things come from within and defile the man.

(Mark 7:21-23)

They did not destroy the nations, concerning whom the Lord commanded them, but were mingled among the heathen, and learned their works. And they served idols which were a snare unto them.

(Psa. 106:34-36)

church regularly, giving more to the poor, fasting, etc.

Pastor Karabo: My son, there is only one way to do things right, that is by doing things God's way.

Tumelo: I've wasted my time and efforts doing garbage instead of taking responsibility and accountability for allowing wealth to take God's place in

For we walk by faith, not by sight.

(2 Cor. 5:7)

That Christ may dwell in your heart by faith, that ye being rooted and grounded in Love.

(Eph. 3:17)

But she that liveth in pleasure is dead while she liveth.

1 tim 5; 6

my life. I thought if I try those other things, I can get away with it.

Pastor Karabo: No one can fool God. You are only deceiving or fooling yourself if you think you can bribe God with your pseudo good works or your religious practice which have nothing to do with Christianity.

Tumelo: I have been a fool!

Be not deceived, God cannot be mocked. What a man sows this he will also reap.

(Gal 6:7)

Therefore because you are lukewarm, in fact neither hot nor cold, I am about to vomit you out of mouth.

(Rev. 3:16)

Fathers shall not be put to death for their children, nor children be put to death for their fathers, each is to die for his own sin.

(Deut. 24:16)

Pastor Karabo: You have been religious. You see, Christianity is not religion. Religion is man's attempt to gain God's approval according to man's approbation or prescription. This is the system which Satan uses to destruct God's children from serving God or living a Christian life instead of a religious life based on

And not many days after, the younger son gathered all together, and took his journey into a far country and there wasted his substance with riotous living.

(Luke 15:13)

If we say that we have no sin, we deceive ourselves, and the truth is not in us.

(1 John 1:8)

Wherefore seeing we also are compassed about with so great a cloud of witness, let us lay aside every weight, and the sin which doth so easily beset us, and let us run with patience the race that is set before us.

(Heb. 12:1)

human good instead of divine good, by focusing on hypocritical acts such as fasting, praying in tongues, paying 10 percent, prophecy, healing, etc.

Tumelo: Really, I've wasted my time and have caused my wealth and good health.

Pastor Karabo: Christianity is based on the basic principle that Christ has done it all and there is nothing

And when he had spent all, there arose a mighty famine in the land, and he began to be in want.

(Luke 15:14)

And he went and joined himself to a citizen of that country, and he sent him into his fields to feed swine.

(Luke 15:15)

And he would fain have filled his belly with the husks that the swine did eat, and no man gave unto him.

(Luke 15:16)

that you and I can do to add to what he has accomplished. Christ died for our past, present, and future sins. Therefore, we are forgiven by acknowledging our sins privately to God the Father, in the name of Christ in the power of God the Holy Spirit and not our good works, which we perform foolishly, thinking that they will make God forgive us or

And when he came to himself, he said, how many hired servants of my father's have bread enough and to spare, and I perish with hunger.

(Luke 15:17)

I will arise and go to my father, and will say unto him, father, I have sinned against heaven, and before thee.

(Luke 15:18)

Believe on the Lord Jesus Christ, and thou shall be saved.

(Acts 16:31)

remove our misfortunes.

Tumelo: Thinking of it, the Lord has been kind to me for not taking everything including whatever is still remaining.

Pastor Karabo: My son, considering things you have done behind God's back, doubting him, not acknowledging your faults, and taking responsibility

It was meet that we should make mercy, and be glad, for thy brother was dead, and is alive again, was lost and is found.

(Luke 15:32)

For to be carnally minded is death, but to be spiritually minded is life and peace; for if ye live after the flesh, ye shall die, but if ye through the spirit do mortify the dead of the body, ye shall live.

(Rom. 8:6-13)

But as soon as this thy son was come, which hath devoured thy living with harlots, thou hast killed for him the fatted calf.

(Luke 15:30)

for your mess, I can confidently say that he has been gracious to you and has been patient, forgiving, merciful, faithful, and loving to not have let you suffer even more from your own doing and self-destruction.

Tumelo: Now that I know I'm to blame for most of the stuff. How do I know when it

Wherefore he saith, awake thou that sleepest, and arise from the dead and Christ shall give the light.

(Eph. 5:14)

And your feet shod with the preparation of the gospel of peace, above all, taking the shield of faith, where with ye shall be able to quench all the fiery don't of the wicked.

(Eph. 6:15-16)

Brethren, I count not myself to have apprehended, but this one thing I do, forgetting those things which are behind, and reaching forth unto those things which are before, I press toward the mark for the prize of high calling of God in Christ Jesus.

(Phil 3:13-14)

is not me who is responsible for my misfortunes? How do I know if it is Satan? How do I know if it is God?

Pastor Karabo: As I have already said, tomorrow we start with Satan and his possible role in your misfortunes.

Tumelo: See you then.

Pastor Karabo: "Good night."

Laugher is good medicine.

(Epigram)

It is a great art to laugh at your suffering.

(Epigram)

The way out of a difficulty is through it.

(Epigram)

Chapter 3

Satan and His Tricks

Pastor Karabo: We meet again in this cold morning. Today I have prepared you a hot vegetable soup.

Tumelo: Lovely! I also brought homemade bread.

Pastor Karabo: I hope you are well this morning and ready to roll.

Tumelo: I could not wait to explore and see what could Satan have done to my situation, and

This is the devil's world.

(2 Cor. 4:4)

Pride comes before the fall.

(Epigram)

Resist the devil and he will flee.

(James 4:7)

I spent hours last night reflecting and writing a list of things I did wrong and am accountable for, and I started praying and asking God to forgive me and accept me back into his fellowship like the prodigal son.

Pastor Karabo: The Lord has long forgiven you. Even as you were praying, he already heard and answered your prayer. God loves you and still has a wonderful

And everyone who keeps having this hope in him purifies himself just as that unique person is pure.

(1 John 3:3)

And it shall come to pass, that before they call, I will answer, and while they are yet speaking, I will hear.

(Isa. 65:24)

He who believes in the son has eternal life, but he who does not obey the son shall not see life, but the wrong of God abide on him.

(John 3:36)

plan for your life.

Tumelo: Do you think God will give me another chance? I am worried that he has lost interest in me. I fear for my health and life.

Pastor Karabo: The fact that you are still alive means that he loves you and still has a wonderful plan for your life.

Tumelo: I pray he forgives me. I pray he

And I give unto them eternal life, and they shall never, perish, neither shall any man pluck them out of my hand.

(John 10:28)

For whom the Lord loveth he chasteneth and scourgeth every son whom he receiveth.

Heb 12; 6

Wherefore lift up the hands which hang down and the feeble knees and make trough paths for your feet, lest that which is lame be turned out of the way, but let it rather be healed.

(Heb. 12:12-13)

gives me another chance. I pray he saves my life and restores my health, and I pray and yearn for fellowship with him.

Pastor Karabo: I can assure you, the Lord will not reject you if you acknowledge your sins. He has heard your prayer, because he is merciful and gracious.

And he arose, and come to his father, but when he was yet a great way off, his father saw him, and had compassion, and ran, and fell on his neck and kisses him.

(Luke 15:20)

I love the Lord, because he hath heard my voice and my supplications. Because he hath inclined his ears unto me, therefore will I call upon him as long as I live.

(Ps. 116:1-2)

Let us therefore come boldly unto the throne of grace, that we may obtain mercy and find grace to help in time of need.

Heb. 4:16

Tumelo: Today I would love to pray as we are about to explore Satan and his tricks in all that I went through and am still experiencing.

Pastor Karabo: Not in tongues, please!

Tumelo: Ha-ha! Very funny.

Pastor Karabo: Shall we get to it?

Tumelo: Certainly! Heavenly Father, we are grateful this morning because of your grace and time

We can be blessed right under the devil's nose.

(Epigram)

God has an amazing sense of humour as he uses ordinary people to show his power.

(Epigram)

Dig your well before you are thirsty

(Epigram)

to try find answers under the teaching of the Holy Spirit to understand what tricks, what role has the devil played to distract me from your plan for my life! We ask all this in Christ's name, our Lord. Amen.

Pastor Karabo: Well done, Tumelo. From a list of your misfortunes I chose control system, security,

God has given His word to adapt to all different times.

(Epigram)

It is of the Lord's mercies that we are not consumed, because his compassions fail not. They are new every morning, great is thy faithfulness.

(Rom. 3:22-23)

The best way out of a problem is through it.

(Epigram)

cash flow reports, how you were managing your debts, expenses, liabilities, profits, and impulsive buying of broken trucks to show you how you were avoiding to take responsibility and accountability for your wrong decisions and instead of blaming it on God and partly blaming it on Satan. But eventually you

Garments of righteousness never go out of style, where no thirst for righteousness the sermon is always dry.

(Epigram)

God never alters the rope of righteous but alters you to righteousness.

(Epigram)

Most people favour righteousness otherwise many would never pretend to have it.

(Epigram)

realize your shortcomings and decided to account for the obvious mess you created for yourself. Right?

Tumelo: Right.

Pastor Karabo: Great! Now, Satan has his own plan, strategy to distract us from serving or living a spiritual life based on glorifying Christ, realizing God's grace, mercy, and faithfulness. Furthermore, to try and deny unbelievers

When you are young, you run into difficulties but when you are old, difficulties run into you.

(Epigram)

The devil's greatest weapon is to inflict fear to believers.

(Epigram)

Life is full of hard knocks but answer them all because one day you will find an opportunity.

(Epigram)

the opportunity to accept Christ as their Lord and Savior. Instead, his strategy is to use or encourage believers to focus on self-glorification, self-focus for giving, praying, healing, and prophesying, tithing, and laws rather than focusing on the grace of God, his mercies, and undeserved blessings. He encourages men to save themselves through their own good works and not focus on the free work of Christ on the cross. He uses fear, doubt, and wealth to control us. His main

Fear not tomorrow , God is already there.

(Epigram)

Swim with the sharks without being eaten alive.

(Epigram)

Knowing that a man is not justified by the works of the law, but by the faith of Jesus Christ, even we have believed in Jesus Christ, that we might be justified by the faith of Christ, and not by the works of the law, for by the works of the law, shall no flesh be justified.

(Gal. 2:16)

focus of areas is to attack our wealth, health, our lives, or those of our families.

Tumelo: You have said a mouthful, and I am falling behind on my notes.

Pastor Karabo: Then we will take it slow.

Tumelo: Without deviating, you seem to have a problem with the good that man does.

Pastor Karabo: Absolutely not!

Tumelo: Clarity then!

Remember, we consider blessed those who have endured. You have heard of the perseverance of Job and you have seen the conclusion brought about by the Lord, because the Lord is full of compassion and mercy.

(James 5:11)

The Lord is not slow about His promise, as some count slowness, but is patient toward you, not wishing for any to perish but for all to come to repentance.

(2 Pet. 3:9)

Job replied, you are talking like a foolish woman. Shall we accept good from God and not trouble?

(Job 2:10)

Pastor Karabo: Of course. God is only interested in divine good and not human good.

Tumelo: What's the difference, Pastor?

Pastor Karabo: The right thing must be done the right way! The wrong thing done the wrong way is obviously wrong, and the right thing done the wrong way is still wrong!

Tumelo: What is the right way?

Pastor Karabo: Everything we do, giving, praying, compassion, helping the sick, going to church, loving our families, friends, neighbors, pure thoughts,

Just over a hill there is a beautiful valley, but you have to climb the hill to see the beauty.

(Epigram)

Suffering is the quickest diet to reduce a fat head.

(Epigram)

For I testify that according to their ability, and beyond their ability, they gave of their own accord.

(2 Cor. 8:3)

behavior, etc., should be for the glorification of God, appreciation and recognition of grace, mercy, and God's faithfulness in our lives and not for our own selfish desires or self-glorification or intention to bribe God in order to have our way. The right way is only God's way and nothing else.

Tumelo: So that's what you mean by divine good.

Pastor Karabo: Human good is based on religion, and religion being nothing but man's attempt or Satan's strategy to encourage man to serve God according to his own prescription and not according to the Word of God.

Tumelo I see!

Pastor Karabo: Instead of taking responsibility

For by grace ye saved through faith, and that not of yourselves, it is the gift of God, not of works, lest any man should boast.

(Eph. 2:8-9)

For such is the will of God that by doing good, you may silence the ignorance of foolish men.

(1 Pet. 2:15)

Without faith, you will never have courage to lose sight of the land nor discover new oceans.

(Epigram)

for your sin of backsliding, you resorted to other things.

Tumelo: I know.

Pastor Karabo: Let's take one of your misfortunes which we can't hold you responsible or accountable for.

Tumelo: Yes.

Pastor Karabo: When your beautiful, aggressive machine, your Dodge Nitro, was stolen at dealer, surely we can't blame you because you had no control over what was coming. You couldn't have known that your car was going to be stolen at that dealer,

Nothing in life happens by accident.

(Epigram)

Adversity in your life, maybe prosperity in disguise.

(Epigram)

Once more the devil transported Him to a very high vantage point and showed Him the kingdoms of the world and their glamor.

(Matt. 4:8)

right?

Tumelo: Right!

Pastor Karabo: There you can hold Satan responsible for sending evil men to steal your car and God for permitting it.

Tumelo: I knew it.

Pastor Karabo: Don't be so excited because you did things which might have contributed to you losing that car and other misfortunes.

Tumelo: How?

Pastor Karabo: After God blessed you with your car, you decided to go to the cemetery and thank your dead parents, and when other misfortunes came, you started consulting the spiritualist,

Then he said to Him, all of these I will give to You, if You fall down and worship me.

(Matt. 4:9)

And satan said to Jesus, if you are the Son of God, jump, For it stands written, God will command His angels concerning you, and they will lift you up in their hands so that you will not strike foot against a stone.

(Matt. 4:6)

The heart is deceitful above all things, and desperately wicked.

(Jer. 17:9)

using candles, oils, pseudo tongues, fasting, pseudo giving, and allowing yourself to be washed with chicken's blood and doing all these demonic practices, which promoted Satan's desires and have no place in God's plan.

Tumelo: I am so ashamed. I deserve to die. I wish I could reverse the clock and undo my mess.

Pastor Karabo: Instead of confessing your sins for backsliding, getting back into fellowship, studying the Word of God and seeking answers, you exposed yourself to all these rituals of religion, which worsened your situation, instead of faith in your God.

And when Saul enquired of the Lord, the Lord answered him not, neither by dreams, nor by urim, nor by prophets.

(1 Sam 28:6)

For all have sinned, and came short of the glory God.

(Rom. 3:23)

And the son said unto him, Father I have sinned against heaven, and in thy sight, and am no, more worthy to be called thy son.

(Luke 15:21)

Tumelo: What a mess!

Pastor Karabo: What a choice!

Tumelo: And Satan?

Pastor Karabo: Every time God blesses us, Satan argues that we serve God because of those blessing, but as soon as they are gone, we will turn against God. But God disagrees and argues that we will serve, trust, and fear him even if Satan takes our blessing.

Tumelo: So there is a constant battle to prove who's right.

Pastor Karabo: "Correct!"

The Lord said to Satan, very well, then, everything he has is in your hands, but on the man himself do not lay a finger.

(Job 1:12)

And he said, naked I came from my mother's womb, and naked i will depart. The Lord gave and the Lord has taken away, may the name of the Lord be praised.

(Job 1:21-22)

I know that my redeemer lives, and that in the end he will stand upon the earth. After my skin has been destroyed, yet in my flesh I will see God.

(Job 19:25-26)

Pastor Karabo: Satan uses lots of tricks to try and prove his point. He knows that judgment waits for him, and he is not willing to go down the drain alone.

Tumelo: Can you tell me some of those tricks?

Pastor Karabo: He uses fear, doubt, wealth, health, and death to gain power and control over man, and he presents tempting situations and capitalize on man's own selfish desire from our own sin nature.

Tumelo: Still curious about more tricks!

Pastor Karabo: OK. Instead

For we wrestle not against flesh and blood, but against principalities against power, against the rules of the darkness of this world, against spiritual wickedness in high places.

(Eph. 6:12)

For that which i do, i allow not.

(Rom. 7:15)

Resist the devil and he will flee.

(James 4:7)

of focusing on the answers from the Word of God (the Bible) when we face crisis, we resort to evil things to try and find solutions or get certainty that the future will be better or what should we do to make it better or influence it or change it by ourselves. So we end up consulting the dead, stars, fortune-tellers, spiritual healers, idols such as animals, wood, trees, sun, fire, voodoos, water, cross, certain people, and ourselves, etc.

Tumelo: I'm not innocent.

Pastor Karabo: Though I hold you

Therefore because you are luke warm, in fact neither hot nor cold, i am about to vomit you out of my mouth.

(Rev. 3:16)

He day a grave and explored it therefore he has fallen into a ditch which he himself has constructed. His frustration shall return on his own head.

(Ps. 7:15-16)

For this reason, many are weak and sick and a number of believers sleep, but if we would judge ourselves, we should not be judged.

(1 Cor. 11:30-31)

responsible for most of the wrong decisions and choices you made, but the situation for your losses or misfortunes were brought about by Satan and his demons, and the people used in the process such as your staff, former PA, and her husband were used by him to try and destroy you, to instill fear, doubt with a hope that you will turn against your God and worship Satan.

Tumelo: I feel like I did serve Satan!

Pastor Karabo: To a great extent you allowed him and his demons to influence you and lost your

No testing has overtaken you but such as is common to mankind, but God is faithful, who will not permit you to be tested beyond what you are able, but with testing will also provide a solution that you may be able to endure it

(1 Cor. 10:13)

Fathers shall not be put to death for their children, nor children be put to death for their fathers, each is to die for his own sin.

(Deut. 24:16)

Let the wicked forsake his way, and the unrighteous man his thoughts, and he will have mercy upon him and to our God, for he will abundantly pardon.

(Isa. 55:7)

focus, and he used the wealth God gave you to distract you from serving your God.

Tumelo: So Satan tempts us?

Pastor Karabo: Though true, we still have a choice. Satan has no power over your choice. You still decided to fall for his temptation. If you resist him, he will flee. Sometimes, even if it is not Satan tempting us, our own sin or own selfish desire may tempt us. He uses his demons to influence believers who are out of fellowship or backsliding and also encourages the unbelievers to

Satan answered the Lord, and said, doth Job fear God for nought? Hast not thou made a hedge about him, and about his house, and about all that he hath on every side? Thou hast blessed the work of his hands; his substance is increasing in the land. But put faith thine hand now and touch all that he hath and he will curse thee to thy face.

(Job 1:10-11)

And the Lord said unto Satan, hast thou considered my servant Job that there is none like him in the earth; a perfect and an upright man, that fearth God, and shuns evil? And still he holdeth fast his integrity, although thou movedst me against him, to destroy him without cause.

(Job 2:3)

And Satan answered the Lord, and said, skin for skin, yea, all that a man hath will he give for his life, but put forth thine hand now and touch his bone and his flesh, and he will curse thee to thy face.

(Job 2:4-5)

reject the Gospel or Christ as their only savior or solution. He infiltrates our minds through mental sins like jealous, envy, fear, lust, power and sins from our mouth like gossiping, judging, spreading rumors, instigating conflict, and physical sins like unfaithfulness, stealing, murder, etc.

And this is the record that God hath given to us eternal life, and this life is in his son.

(1 John 5:11)

For I am persuaded, that neither death nor life, no angels, nor principalities, nor power, nor things present, nor things to come nor height, nor depth, nor any other creature shall be able to separate us from the love of God, which is in Christ Jesus our Lord.

(Rom 8:38-39)

And I give unto them eternal life, and they shall never perish, neither shall any man.

(John 10:28)

Tumelo: But can man win this fight?

Pastor Karabo: I will come back to your question, but I firstly want to stress the fact that Satan also uses our cultures, rituals, race, and languages to distract us from changing everything we were taught at home, school, and in our community for Christ's sake.

Tumelo: Do we have to stop following our cultures when we become believers in Christ ?

Pastor Karabo: Culture is a good thing for self-determination as a nation or tribe, but

Wherefore be ye not unwise, but understand what the will of the Lord is.

(Eph. 5:14)

See then that ye walk circumspectly, not as fools, but as wise.

(Eph. 5:15)

For as he thinketh in his heart, so is he.

(Prov. 23:7)

anything that takes God's place in your life such as worshipping the dead, animals, wood, trees, cross, water, or any form of practice other than the fact that we are saved by grace and not by our good works. Christ is the only way to serve God, period! Anything other than salvation through Christ is religion and has no place in God's plan. You need to choose. You can't serve God and other gods or idols or rituals.

For we walk by faith, not by sight.

(2 Cor. 5:7)

My little children, of whom i travail in birth again until Christ be formed in you.

(Gal 4:19)

You shall not make for yourself on idol, or any likeness of what is in heaven above or on earth beneath or in the water under the earth. You shall not worship them or serve them, for i the Lord your God; am a jealous God, visiting the iniquity of the fathers on the children, on the third and fourth generation of those who hate me.

(Exod. 20:4-5)

Tumelo: But can we really win?

Pastor Karabo: We have already won by acknowledging that when Christ went to the cross, he died for every possible sin in our bones and souls. Christ has done it all, and there is nothing that you and I can add or omit to what he has accomplished. We are saved by grace alone in Christ Jesus, and it is the same grace and mercy that sustain us on earth till death and after then.

For that which i do, i allow not, for what i would, that do i not, but what i hate, that do I.

(Rom. 7:15)

Behold, happy is the man when God reproves, therefore, do not despise the discipline of El Shaddoi, for he inflicts pain and he bondages the wound.

(Job 5:17-18)

Believe on the Lord Jesus Christ and thou shall be saved.

(Acts 16:31)

Tumelo: So we can conclude that all my misfortunes were brought about by Satan with the aim that he distracts me from serving, fearing, and glorifying my God!

Pastor Karabo: Tumelo, remember you learned and acknowledged that you were responsible for some or most of your mess or misfortunes, right?

Tumelo: Correct.

Pastor Karabo: Satan benefited from your wrong decisions and used his influence or demonic forces to take away all that the Lord has blessed you

Once more the devil transported him to a very high vantage point and showed him all the kingdoms of the world and their glamour.

(Matt. 4:8)

For the wrath of man shall praise thee.

(Ps. 76:10)

My people are destroyed for lack of knowledge. Because you have rejected knowledge, i also will reject you from being my priest. Since you have forgotten the law of your God, i also will forget your children.

(Hosea 4:6)

with your wealth and your health to make you live in fear and have doubt in your loving God. All he wants is for you to have fear and not trust and serve your God. Instead he wants you turn against your God.

Tumelo: So how do I recover from this? How do I overpower Satan?

Pastor Karabo: You have already started by taking responsibility and accounting that the choices and decisions made by you, not Satan or God, contributed to your misfortunes.

And the Lord said unto Satan, whence comest thou? Then Satan answered the Lord and said from going to and from in the earth, and from walking up and down in it.

(Job 1:7)

If we confess our sins, he is faithful and just to forgive us our sins and purify us from all unrighteousness.

(1John 1:9)

Grow in the grace and knowledge of our Lord and saviour Jesus Chris. To him is the glory, both now and to the doing of eternity.

(2 Pet. 3:18)

Tumelo: I have overcome myself from self-destruction, but now how do I overcome Satan?

Pastor Karabo: You overcame him the day you accepted Christ as your Lord and Savior! The question you are trying to ask is, while on earth, now that Christ has died for your sins, past, present, and future, how do you deal with the influence, tricks, and tests that Satan brings to you?

Tumelo: You have hit a nail on the head!

He saved us, not on the basis of deeds which we have done in righteousness, but according to his mercy, by the washing of regeneration and renewing by the Holy Spirit.

As many as received him, to them gave the power to become the sons of God, even to them that believe on his name.

(John 1:12)

I say unto you, that likewise joy shall be in heaven over one sinner that repenteth, more than over ninety and nine just persons, which need no repentance.

(Luke 15:7)

Pastor Karabo: "Dealing with Satan is not impossible but also not as easy as taking responsibility for your decisions, choices, and your free will. Satan is a very intelligent creature or a former angel who was blessed by God with wisdom and power, which was intended for the divine good and the glorification and worship of God the Father, the Son, the Holy Spirit. But as you know, greed, power, and envy made Satan proud, and he wanted to be God, so he was dismissed, and he left with his powers, wisdom, and demons,

> If I cast out devil by the spirit of God then the kingdom of God is come unto you.
>
> (Matt. 12:28)

> For from within out of the heart of men, proceed evil thoughts, adulteries, fornications, murders, thefts, covetousness, wickedness, deceit, lasciviousness, on evil eye, blasphemy, pride, foolishness, all these evil things come from within and defile the man.
>
> (Mark 7:21-23)

> For this purpose the son of God was manifested, that he might destroy the works of the devil.
>
> (1 John 3:8)

which he now uses to the maximum to distract man from serving and glorifying God!

Tumelo: A cup of tea?

Pastor Karabo: Yes, please.

Tumelo: I'm listening.

Pastor Karabo: His power, wisdom, and demons are now used to try and destroy man through his strategies, witchcraft, religion, false miracle workers, false tongues, false healing, human sacrifice, drinking of animals' blood, sleeping with animals, idol, enticement, stealing, killing, rebellion, false giving, idols, worship moon, stars, dreams, false teachers,

A man also or a woman that hath a familiar spirit or that is a wizard, shall surely be put to death, they shall stone them with stones, their blood shall be upon them.

(Lev. 20:27)

For all that do these things are an abomination unto the Lord, and because of these abominations the Lord thy God doth drive them out from before thee.

(Duet. 18:12)

When the enemy shall come in like a flood the spirit of the Lord shall lift up a standard against him.

(Isa. 59:19)

false prophecy, claims of casting out demons, fear, doubt, success, materialism, alcohol abuse, drugs, etc. And with all that said, God's love has created a plan, a divine plan for man to beat Satan in his own game, and God's plan has been created to deal with sin and for the glorification of God through Christ Jesus and for man to be blessed while on earth, right under the devil's nose, in the midst of all his tricks and evil ways.

Tumelo: Wonderful, but where do I start?

And Satan said to Jesus, if you are the son of God, jump, for it stands written, he will command his angels concerning you, and they will lift you up in their hands so that you will not strike your foot against a stone.

(Matt. 4:6)

Then Satan said to Jesus, all of these i will give to you, if you fall down and worship me.

(Matt. 4:9)

Jesus replied to him once more, do not put the Lord your God to the test.

(Matt. 4:7)

Pastor Karabo: We start by going back to your misfortunes to understand why would God allow these misfortunes if he loves you so much.

Tumelo: Is that for tomorrow?

Pastor Karabo: "My son, I have lost track of time. I did not realize how late it is.

Tumelo: Can we start a little bit earlier?

Pastor Karabo: How is eight o'clock for you?

Tumelo: Perfect! Good night!

The fear of the Lord is the beginning of wisdom.

(Prov. 1:7)

Then Jesus said to him, go, Satan, for it stands written worship the Lord your God, serve him only.

(Matt. 4:10)

Then the devil left him, and behold angels came to him and began to serve him

(Matt. 4: 11)

Chapter 4

God and His Grace

Tumelo: Greetings, Mrs. Mosa!

Mrs. Mosa: Greetings, Tumelo. I have not seen you in a long time.

Tumelo: I have not seen you too. I have been here and there, mostly busy with business challenges.

Pastor Karabo: Morning, Tumelo.

Tumelo: Morning, Pastor!

Pastor Karabo: You remember my wife, don't you?

Tumelo: Of course, Pastor!

Mrs. Mosa: Husband, have you forgotten

But he that glorieth, let him glory in the Lord.

(2 Cor. 10:17)

For not he that commendeth himself is approved, but whom the Lord commendeth.

(2 Cor. 10:18)

David said moreover, The Lord that delivered me out of the power of the lion, and out of the power of the bear, he will deliver me out of the hand of this Philistine.

(1 Sam. 17:37)

that Tumelo was one of the first students in my Sunday school class when we started this church?

Pastor Karabo: Wifey, I have forgotten. This young man started with us when we started this ministry?

Mrs. Mosa: The Lord has been good to us.

Pastor Karabo: Indeed.

Tumelo: You have been consistent in serving the Lord in this community.

Pastor Karabo: It has not been easy, but by God's grace, we are still here!

Mrs Mosa: "Grace all the way, my husband."

For by grace are ye saved through faith, and that not of yourselves, it is the gift God ; Not of works, lest any man should boast.

(Eph. 2:8-9)

Thou wilt keep me in perfect peace whose mind is stayed on thee, because he trusteth in thee.

(Isa. 26:3)

For the weapons of our warfare are not carnal, but mighty through God to the pulling down of strong holds.

(2 Cor. 10:4)

Pastor Karabo: In all these years, we have seen everything with our own eyes. We have heard it all and understood it.

Mrs. Mosa: Tumelo, we have made so many mistakes that we have lost count, but somehow, the Lord has been gracious, merciful, and forgiving. We don't deserve any of the blessings we have, and neither have we earned it, but the hand of God at work has brought us to where we are today.

Tumelo: You, mistakes?

Pastor Karabo: Yes, Tumelo. Yes, my son, I have listened to your

For my thoughts are not your thought, neither are your ways my ways, saith The Lord.

(Isa. 55:8)

For as the heavens are higher than the earth, so are my ways higher than your ways, and my thoughts than your thoughts.

(Isa. 55:9)

Let the wicked forsake his way, the unrighteous man his thoughts; and let him return unto The Lord, and He will have mercy upon him, and to our God, for He will abundantly pardon.

(Isa. 55:7)

stories, and I realize that you are not worse than I was. We have messed up many times and worse so in the ministry and in personal life because of lack of doctrine and the Word of God in our souls.

Mrs. Mosa: How I wish we could undo our mess, especially were we lost people who needed hope, the truth, the Word of God but got garbage because of our backsliding, lack of doctrine, focus on egos, and desire for power and control in the church.

Pastor Karabo: Tumelo, we focused on pleasing and gaining approval of people to try and win

For the one who sows to his own flesh shall from the flesh reap corruption.

(Gal. 6:7-8)

If we name our sins, He is faithful and absolute righteousness to forgive us the sins we name and to purify us from all wrongdoing.

(1 John 1:9)

But if we judge ourselves rightly, we should not be judged.

(1 Cor. 11:29-31)

them to our church. We focused on increasing numbers in the church instead of teaching the Word of God and allowing him to change lives. The focus was on us and not God.

Tumelo: How did you overcome!

Mrs. Mosa: "Just like you, because of our backsliding, we experienced God's stick and from the pain realized that we were serving Satan and his tricks.

Pastor Karabo: We had to start studying the Word of God (the Bible) word by word, verse by verse, line by line on a daily basis. I started teaching doctrine

The right thing done the wrong way, is wrong, the right thing must be done the right way.

(Epigram)

For they sow the wind, and they reap the whirlwind.

(Hosea 8:7)

All scripture is God-breathed, and is profitable for doctrine, for reproof, for correction, for instruction in righteousness, that the man of God might be mature, thoroughly furnished unto all good works.

(2 Tim. 3:16-17)

and no longer focused on garbage, which promoted religion and Satan's agenda.

Tumelo: Then what happened?

Pastor Karabo: We lost members because we were no longer licking their rear but started redirecting their focus on grace, which had no room for their pseudo good works or desire for recognition.

Mrs Mosa: From hundred and twenty, we were left with just under ten members, who remained loyal to the true teachings of the Word of God.

Tumelo: So there is hope for me to recover from my mess?

What shall we then say to these things? If God be for us, who can be against us?

(Rom. 8:31)

For what the law could not do, in that it was weak through the flesh, God sending His own Son in the likeness of sinful flesh and for sin, condemned sin in the flesh.

(Rom. 8:3)

That the righteousness of the law might be fulfilled in us, who walk not after the flesh, but after the Spirit.

(Rom. 8:4)

Pastor Karabo: God would have not given you this time, privilege, opportunity to study and hear what he has to say to you if he no longer had any plan for you or your life.

Mrs. Mosa: Tumelo, God helps those who need and ask for his help and not the self-righteous, the perfect, the holy holy, the religious, the judges, the crusaders, the human good workers, etc. Faith is about trust in God. Grace and mercy are about acknowledging that God is the provider and source of everything, our salvation, health, wealth, breath, talents

Contrary to our belief, God help those who need his help and not those who help themselves.

(Epigram)

The Lord has sworn by his right hand and by his mighty arm, never again will I give your grain as for food your enemies, and never again will foreigners drink the new wine for which you have toiled.

(Isa. 62:8)

But my God shall supply all your needs according to his riches in glory by Christ Jesus.

(Phil. 4:19)

food, shelter, safety, rain, peace, happiness, family, friends, etc. Everything comes from God, and him alone deserves the credit and the glory.

Pastor Karabo: We knew that once we focus on the truth, Christianity, the grace of God, his mercy, and the fact that as believers we have to live and walk by faith alone and not sight and not preach or promote religion, we were going to lose members, especially those who were financing this church and wanted the glory. But this is the choice that we had to make, God or man, human good or grace, religion or Christianity.

For with God nothing shall be impossible.

(Luke 1:37)

All things work together for good.

(Rom. 8:28)

Fear thou not for I am with thee.

(Isa. 41:10)

Tumelo: And the numbers started dropping?

Mrs. Mosa: Yes, they did, but it was the best decision we have ever made. We recovered, and so will you.

Tumelo: Thank you!

Mrs. Mosa: I have wasted your time. Let me leave you two to work.

Tumelo: No, you have not. I needed to hear all this.

Pastor Karabo: Before you leave, wifey, do you mind to pray for us?

The battle is the Lord's.

(1 Sam. 17:47)

Casting all your care upon Him, for He careth for you.

But my God shall supply all your needs according to his riches in glory by Christ Jesus.

(Phil 4:19)

Mrs. Mosa: Certainly. Heavenly Father, thank you for your mercy, your grace, and your faithfulness. I pray for Tumelo and Pastor Karabo that through the Holy Spirit they find answers to their challenges and quest for the truth. In Jesus's name. Amen.

Pastor Karabo: Thanks, wifey.

Tumelo: Amen.

Pastor Karabo: As usual, we have to go back to your misfortunes so that we don't side track and that you find all your answers!

Be transformed by the renewing of your mind.

(Rom. 12:2)

Our inner man is being renewed day by day.

(2 Cor. 4:16)

Man shall not live on bread alone but on every word that proceeds out of the mouth of God.

(Matt. 4:4)

Tumelo: OK. But it was interesting to hear you and your wife telling me of your mistakes and how you learned from them.

Pastor Karabo: My son, we have done stupid decisions than you realize, and in ministry and in our private lives. I can go on and on telling you different stories about our flaws and how we refused to account, blaming Satan and at times blaming God, but by grace, the stick from God and the truth from his word challenged and rescued us.

Tumelo: I guess the only way to see a true

If you falter in times of trouble, how small is your faith.

(Prov. 24:10)

Thou wilt keep him in perfect peace whose mind is stayed on thee, because he trusteth in thee.

(Isa. 26:3)

God is our refuge and strength, a very present help in trouble.

(Ps. 46:1)

picture or reflection of yourself is in the Word of God.

Pastor Karabo: Absolutely!

Tumelo: So my solutions are also in God's Word!

Pastor Karabo: Today, you are sober, aren't you?

Tumelo: I need the truth, I need help!

Pastor Karabo: Great! In all that I have heard from your stories, your misfortunes, you losing your car mysteriously, staff stealing your stock, your money and owing every one and the wrong investments you ended up making

Stop being conformed to this age, but be transformed by the renovation of your thought, that you may prove what the will of God is, the good, the well-pleasing, and the complete.

(Rom. 12:2)

Keep on having this mental attitude in you, which was also in Christ Jesus.

(Phil. 2:5)

It is not the absence or the presence of problems that will determine peace in your life, but the absence of the presence of God.

(Epigram)

out of fear and frustration. I can confidently say all that happened, yesterday, today, and still to come, was and is necessary for your good and for the glorification of our Lord Jesus Christ.

Tumelo: I agree.

Pastor Karabo: Though Satan brought misfortunes to try and destroy you, though you also brought suffering upon yourself through wrong decisions, God has allowed it to discipline you so that you may return to him (fellowship) and also that you may mature spiritually through suffering and to strengthen

No testing has overtaken you but such as, is common to mankind; but God is faithful, who will not permit you to be tested beyond what you are able, but with the testing will also provide a solution, that you may be able to endure.

(1 Cor. 10:13)

For this reason I find contentment in weaknesses, in slanders, in pressures, in persecutions, in stresses in behalf of Christ, for when I am weak, then I am powerful.

(2 Cor. 12:10)

For to you it has been given in behalf of Christ not only to believe in Him but also to suffer for his sake.

(Phil. 1:29)

your faith in him, see his grace and mercy upon you, and give him the glory he deserves.

Tumelo: God tore me apart.

Pastor Karabo: Instead of going back to God, confessing your sins, and recovering from backsliding, you opted for human solutions, religious practices such as pseudo tongues, false giving, false prophecy, rituals, idols, etc., in seeking solutions to your problems. The reality of life to both believers and unbelievers is that suffering is certain and comes either to discipline or bless.

For by grace are ye saved through faith, and that not of yourselves; it is the gift of God, Not of works, lest any man should boast.

(Eph. 2:8-9)

For this purpose, the Son of God was manifested, that he might destroy the works of the devil.

(1 John 3:8)

The secret things belong unto the Lord our God, but those things which are revealed belong unto us and to our children for ever, that we may do all the words of this law.

(Deut. 29:29)

Satan brings these sufferings and God allows them for our own good.

Tumelo: How can suffering be good for us?

Pastor Karabo: When you love a child and they are about to burn themselves on a hot plate on the stove, you inflict a lighter pain by smacking them on the hand to save them from burning themselves and teaching them about the danger of a hot plate. When you go to the gym to build muscles, you cannot develop muscles unless you go through

And so you yourselves have forgotten a principle of doctrine which teaches you as sons; My son, do not make light of corrective discipline from the Lord nor be fainting when you are reprimanded by Him.

(Heb. 12:5)

For when the Lord loves He disciplines, and He punishes every son whom He welcomes home.

(Heb. 12:6)

Because of corrective discipline endure.

(Heb. 12:7)

the pain of exercising. Faith life works the same way. It cannot grow unless tested through pain, uncomfortable situations, and challenges.

Tumelo: So pain is good?

Pastor Karabo: Pain may be necessary!

Tumelo: So I can blame God for my suffering?

Pastor Karabo: You can hold him accountable for permitting suffering for the misfortunes caused by your stupidity, arrogance, laziness, and ignorance or misfortunes brought about by Satan to take place.

Tumelo: OK!

Suffering does not always come to injure but provide more opportunities to remind us of the presence of God.

(Epigram)

Behold, happy is the man whom God reproves. Therefore, do not despise the discipline of El-Shaddai, for He inflicts pain and He bandages the wound. He wounds and His hands heal.

(Job 5:17-18)

Therefore, because you are lukewarm, in fact neither hot nor cold, I am about to vomit you out of my mouth.

(Rev. 3:16)

Pastor Karabo: Tumelo, most of the time, we make wrong decisions and yet we never suffer all its consequences because God always intervenes and permits only the suffering we can handle.

Tumelo: So we are on earth to suffer!

Pastor Karabo: We are on earth to serve God and not ourselves or Satan.

Tumelo: Where do I go from here?

Pastor Karabo: We focus on the plan of God for mankind.

And he arose, and came to his father. But when he was yet a great way off, his father saw him, and had compassion and ran and fell on his neck, and kissed him.

(Luke 15:20)

Though He slay me, yet will I trust Him.

(Job 13:15)

Believe on the Lord Jesus Christ, and thou shall be saved.

(Acts 16:31)

Tumelo: Sure!

Pastor Karabo: It is God's will that all mankind become free from sin through the death of Christ on the cross and though he wishes that, he allows us to accept or reject him out of our own free will. The same way Satan and his demons rebelled against God out of their own free will. God wants us to choose him freely and because he loves us went to an extra mile by coming with

same as above (Jesus Christ, the same yesterday, today and forever)

(Heb 13:8)

And there is salvation in no one else; for there is no other name under heaven that has been given among men, by which we must be saved.

(Acts 4:12)

But as many as received Him, to them He gave the right to become children of God, even to those who believe in His name.

(John 1:12)

a plan of salvation, whereby Christ had to die for all our sins, past, present, and future sins and also to cleanse us from all unrighteousness.

Tumelo: All the sins?

Pastor Karabo: All our sins, such as jealousy, anger, bitterness, vindictiveness, implacability, maligning, judging, gossip, stealing, murder, worshipping idols, the dead, stars, water, candles, oils, animals, religious practice, cults, and all sorts of demonic or evil practices, etc. Because Christ died for all these sins so that we may have eternal life.

Tumelo: What about the consequences

He saved us, not on the basis of deeds which we have done in righteousness, but according to His mercy, by the washing of regeneration and renewing by the Holy Spirit.

(Titus 3:5)

He made Him who knew no sin to be sin on our behalf, that we might become the righteousness of God in Him.

(2 Cor. 5:21)

He that spares not His own Son, but delivered Him up for us all, how shall He not with Him also freely give us all things.

(Rom. 8:32)

of our sins while on earth?

Pastor Karabo: The basic rule of life remains for both believers and believers that garbage in, garbage out. If you jump off the cliff, you will die or break your neck whether you are a believer or not. You pay for your sins while on earth through the consequences or the outcome of your sin or foolish decision. Being a believer does not make you immune to nature taking its cause and neither does it mean you now lose your common sense and operate by emotions. And furthermore, it does not

For they sow the wind and they reap the whirlwind.

(Hosea 8:7)

He who sows iniquity will reap vanity.

(Prov. 22:8)

Do not be deceived, God is not mocked, for wherever a man sows, this he will also reap.

(Gal. 6:7)

mean that now that you are a believer in Christ, you no longer sin or have problems.

Tumelo: What is the benefit?

Pastor Karabo: For the unbeliever, the issue is if you accept Christ as your Lord and Savior, then heaven is your home and all your sins will be forgiven and now you are the son of God. As for the believers the issue is to have fellowship with God through acknowledging your sins when you have sinned, studying the Word of God on a daily basis so that you can know the

For that which I do, I allow not; for what I would, that do I not, but what I hate, that do I.

(Rom. 7:15)

Therefore just as through one man sin entered into the world, and death through sin, and so death spread to all men, because all sinned.

(Rom. 5:12)

And He himself bore our sins in His body on the cross, that we might die to sin and live to righteousness, for by His wounds you were healed.

(1 Pet. 2:24)

will of God and can mature spiritually through daily study of the Word and can apply it to any trials, tests, and challenges that will come your way.

Tumelo: So I can deal with my daily sins.

Pastor Karabo: If you have the doctrine in your soul, then you can overcome the evil desires that live within you—mental sins, sins from your mouth, and the overt sins. The Word of God gives you strength to deal with the constant challenges of sin, and furthermore, as a believer, you have direct access to God through prayer. When

Grow in grace and knowledge of our Lord and Saviour Jesus Christ. To Him be the glory both now and to the day of eternity.

(2 Pet. 3:18)

All scripture is God breathed, and is profitable for doctrine, for reproof, for correction, for instruction in righteousness; that the man of God might be mature, thoroughly furnished unto all good works.

(2 Tim. 3:16-17)

Doctrine in your soul, is a panacea, a cure for all, a remedy for everything.

(Epigram)

we study the Word of God, he is talking to us, and when we pray, we are talking to him. The other benefit is that when we are in fellowship with God, God the Holy Spirit is with us to guide us, teach us the word and God's will.

Tumelo: So the Trinity is operational for man's sake?

Pastor Karabo: God the Father created the salvation plan. God the

I urge you therefore, brethren, by the mercies of God, to present your bodies a living and holy sacrifice, acceptable to God, which is your spiritual service of worship.

(Rom. 12:1)

If we confess our sins, He is faithful and righteous to forgive us our sins and to cleanse us from all unrighteousness.

(1 John 1:9)

And do not go presenting the members of your body to sin as instruments of unrighteousness, but present yourselves to God as those alive from the dead, and your members as instruments of righteousness to God.

(Rom. 6:13)

Son executed the plan, and God the Holy Spirit reveals the plan through the Word of God (the Bible).

Tumelo: So I am like Job?

Pastor Karabo: No, you are not. You deserve most of your suffering and more. Wealth made you backslide. The Word of God was no longer important to you, and when misfortunes came,

Go ye therefore, and teach all nations, baptizing them in the name of The Father, and of The Son and of The Holy Spirit.

(Matt. 28:19)

For it is better, if God should will it so, that you suffer for doing what is right rather than for doing what is wrong.

(1 Pet. 3:17)

We do not see things as they are but we see things as we are.

(Epigram)

instead of confessing your sins to God and getting back into fellowship with him and trusting that he will deal with your misfortunes in his own way and own time, you resorted to other means to try and resolve your problems. The only similarity between you and Job is that you also lost your wealth and started suffering healthwise.

Tumelo: I know I'm at fault. I know what I should have done.

Pastor Karabo: All you need is to surrender all to God, confess your sins to him, get back into fellowship, study the word daily, and grow in grace."

Tumelo: I have learned

The Word of God is alive and powerful, sharper than any two edged sword, piercing even to the dividing asunder of the soul and the spirit, and of the joints and the marrow, and is a critic of thoughts and intents of the heart.

(Heb. 4:12)

All scripture is God-breathed, and is profitable for doctrine, for reproof, for correction, for instruction in righteousness; that the man of God might be mature, thoroughly furnished unto good works.

(2 Tim. 3:16-17)

Study to show thyself approved unto God, a workman that needeth not to be ashamed, rightly dividing the Word of truth.

(2 Tim. 2:15)

my lessons!

Pastor Karabo: Have you?

Tumelo: God has been gracious to me. I don't deserve even the blessings that still remain!

Pastor Karabo: Then my job is done, but I would like to hear from you about the lessons you say you have learned.

Tumelo: Tomorrow I do the talking, right?

Pastor Karabo: Right. Any questions?

Tumelo: Can you give more information on grace, mercy, and faith versus religion?

God never alters the rope of righteousness but alters you to righteousness.

(Epigram)

He who is wise wins souls.

(Prov. 11:30)

Know that a man is not justified by observing the law, but by faith in Jesus Christ. So we, too have put our faith in Jesus Christ that we may be justified by faith in Christ and not by observing the law, because by observing the law no one will be justified.

(Gal. 2:16)

Pastor Karabo: Then we proceed so that you live with clarity.

Tumelo: Cool!

Pastor Karabo: Religion is man's attempt to serve God according to his own approbation or prescription or human good.

Tumelo: Meaning?

Pastor Karabo: Meaning, man tries to replace the work of Christ on the cross to earn blessings and forgiveness by his efforts and own good works. He says to himself, "If I give tithe,

Religion is man's attempt to serve God by his own prescription or approbation.

(Epigram)

For all of us have become like one who is unclean, and all our righteous deeds are like a filthy garment.

(Isa. 64:6)

For all have sinned and fall short of the glory of God.

(Rom. 3:23)

pray in tongues, believe in prophecies, dreams, visions, follow my culture, keep the Ten Commandments, go to church every Sunday, participate at the church, look after the poor, widows, pay my taxes, then surely this is enough to gain God's forgiveness and blessings. Man wants to resolve his problem of sin according to what he thinks is right or enough to gain God's justice.

Tumelo: And Christianity?

Pastor Karabo: Christianity says all my human works, tongues, tithing, prophecies, dreams, visions, culture, the Ten Commandments, going to church every Sunday, participating

Trust in the Lord with all your heart, And do not lean on your own understanding. In all your ways acknowledge Him, and He will make your paths straight.

(Prov. 3:5-6)

He saved us, not on the basis of deeds which we have done in righteousness, but according to His mercy; by the washing of regeneration and renewing by the Holy Spirit.

(Titus 3:5)

For we walk by faith, not by sight.

(2 Cor. 5:7)

to church, looking after the poor, widows, paying my taxes can't save me or gain God's forgiveness or blessings. Divine good is for the glorification of God.

Tumelo: I'm listening!

Pastor Karabo: Christianity is about grace, mercy, and faith. Grace means not your efforts, undeserved. There is nothing man can do to earn God's grace or mercy. Your forgiveness is only through Christ's death on the cross, your blessings from

For without faith it is impossible to please Him.

(Heb. 11:6)

Staggered not at the promise of God through unbelief; but was strong in faith, giving glory to God, and being fully persuaded that, what He has promised, He was able also to perform.

Rom 4:20-21

Whosoever believeth in Him shall not perish but have ever lasting life.

(John 3:16)

God are as a result of grace or God's love for you. Mercy means exactly what grace is, also undeserved and cannot be earned. God felt pity for man, gave his only Son as a substitute so that man may be forgiven and blessed regardless of his failures or undeserved benefits. Faith means to trust God with every situation no matter how hopeless or impossible it may seem in man's eyes or Satan's. Faith means you believe God knows better and his ways are better than ours and therefore surrender all to him. Faith means believing

Fear thou not, for I am with thee; be not dismayed, for I am thy God; I will strengthen thee; I will help thee; I will uphold thee with the right hand of my righteousness.

(Isa. 41:10)

Casting all your care upon Him, for He careth for you.

(1 Pet. 5:7)

Cast thy burden upon the Lord, and He shall sustain thee; He shall never suffer the righteous to be moved.

(Ps. 55:22)

in the outcome before it happens. It also means walking without sight but confident that all will be well because of hope and trust in God. Christianity is based on faith and not our good works, efforts to try rectify or make everything right. It is impossible to please God without faith. Christian life is based on confessing your sins, studying the Word of God, and growing in grace and having fellowship with God while on earth

He that spared not His own Son, but delivered Him for us all, how shall He not with Him also freely give us all things.

(Rom. 8:32)

These things I have spoken unto you, that in me ye might have peace. In the world ye shall have tribulation, but be of good cheer, I have overcome the world.

(John 16:33)

The Word of God liveth and abideth forever.

(1 Pet. 1:23)

Furthermore, Christians have access to God through his word and when they pray to him and the presence of God the Holy Spirit who teaches, guides, and gives power to the believers when they are in fellowship and not backsliding.

Tumelo: Great stuff.

Pastor Karabo: Are you clear now?

Tumelo: Crystal clear!

Pastor Karabo: We meet tomorrow then!

Tumelo: Good night, Pastor.

God is Spirit, and those who warship Him must warship in spirit and truth.

(John 4:24)

I urge you therefore, brethren, by the mercies of God, to present your bodies a living and holy sacrifice, acceptable to God, which is your spiritual service of warship.

(Rom. 12:1)

And do not be conformed to this world, but be transformed by the renewing of your mind, that you may prove what the will of God is, that which is good and acceptable.

(Rom. 12:2)

Chapter 5

Lessons Learned

Tumelo: Morning, Pastor!

Pastor Karabo: Morning, young man.

Tumelo: I want to take this opportunity to thank you from the bottom of my heart for making time to help me find the truth, to help me come to terms with reality, humble myself, take responsibility, accountability, and furthermore see and appreciate the grace of God.

Pastor Karabo: My son, all the glory to God for showing you how much he loves you.

For whom the Lord loveth he chasteneth, and scourgeth every son whom he receiveth.

(Heb. 12:6)

And when he came to himself, he said, how many hired servants of my father's have bread enough and to spare, and I perish with hunger.

(Luke 15:17)

I arise and go to my father, and will say unto him, Father I have sinned against heaven and before thee.

(Luke 15:18)

Tumelo: Sir, I have learned a lot in a short space of time and thank you for your patience and support. I have learned that I am responsible and accountable for my choices. I know that you pay for your sins while on earth, not only after death or judgment. Whether a believer or not, you pay for your mess. The basic rule remains garbage in, garbage out. If I make wrong decisions, I will suffer or go through the consequences of my decisions. God does not interfere with my free will, my decisions but holds me responsible and accountable for those decisions.

For that which I do, I allow not, for what I would, that do I not, but what I hate, that do I.

(Rom. 7:15)

And not many days after, the younger son gathered all together, and took his journey into a far country, and there wasted his substance with riotous living.

(Luke 15:13)

If we say that we have no sin, we deceive ourselves, and the truth is not in us.

(1 John1:8)

Pastor Karabo: Good!

Tumelo: I now understand the difference between religion and Christianity.

Pastor Karabo: What is the difference?

Tumelo: When I'm religious, I focus on me and not God. My motives, my choices, my decisions are for self-glorification, self-gratification, and for my own selfish desires. My focus is on my human good works performed to try and gain God's approval or bribe him with the good that I do. I know now that it is religion and not Christianity that promote pseudo good works, false giving, false tongues, false tithing,

The battle is the Lord's.

(1 Sam. 17:47)

And be not conformed to this world, but be ye transformed by the renewing of your mind, that ye may prove what is that good, and acceptable and perfect, will of God.

(Rom. 12:2)

If ye then be risen with Christ, seek those things which are above, where Christ sitteth on the right hand of God. Set your affection on things above, not on things on the earth.

(Col. 3:1-2)

prophecy, claims of casting out of demons, chasing wealth, consulting the dead, spiritualists, idols, candles, oils, the sun, trees, water, crosses, stars, cards, moons, symbols, signs, animals, worshiping certain people, etc.

Pastor Karabo: Impressive! And Christianity?

Tumelo: Christianity is based on the basic rule that man is weak and can't save himself. Christ came for man's rescue by taking the punishment for man's sins, past, present, and future. Christ has also died for all unrighteousness such as religion, human good such as false giving, false tithing, psuedo tongues,

But without faith, it is impossible to please Him.

(Heb. 11:6)

Jesus Christ, the same, yesterday, today and forever.

(Heb. 13:8)

For we walk by faith, not by sight.

(2 Cor. 5:7)

false prophecy, etc. Man can't do anything to save himself. We are saved by grace, and grace means we don't earn it nor deserve it. Christianity means Christ has done it all, and my efforts can't help but faith, mercy, and the grace of God is the key. After accepting Christ as your Lord and Savior, the next step is to study the Word of God (the Bible) on a daily basis so that you can learn all that God wants you to know about him and an opportunity to apply his word in your life. If or when I sin, I have to confess

Whosoever believeth in Him shall not perish but have everlasting life.

(John 3:16)

Ye are the sons of God by faith in Christ Jesus.

(Gal. 3:26)

But my God shall supply all your needs according to his riches in glory by Christ Jesus.

Phil. 4:19

my sin to God privately, and I will be back into fellowship to receive more doctrine and gospel so that I may grow or mature spiritually in grace and so that I may glorify, trust, and worship God alone. I have learned that in this church age or today, God communicates with us through his word (the Bible) and we communicate back through prayer.

Pastor Karabo: What about the unbelievers?

Tumelo: The issue is, they have to be saved first through Christ and they shall be saved

Fellowship means the word of God is allowed to judge, correct and influence our thoughts, tongues and behaviors.

(Epigram)

But grow in the grace and knowledge of our Lord and Savior Jesus Christ.

(2 Pet. 3:18)

Believe in the Lord Jesus, and you shall be saved.

(Acts 16:31)

and experience the grace of God while on earth and have assurance that when they die, heaven is their home.

Pastor Karabo: Gee!

Tumelo: I now know that my sufferings maybe caused by me, Satan's tricks, or God permitting it in order to discipline or bless me right under the devil's nose or in the midst of his tricks or evil ways.

Pastor Karabo: Yes?

Tumelo: Yes, if I make wrong decisions, I will suffer. Sometimes Satan will bring suffering to try and prove to God that as soon as he takes away my blessings, I will stop

And He himself bore our sins in His body on the cross.

(1 Pet. 2:24)

In everything give thanks, for this is God's will for you in Christ Jesus.

(1 Thess. 5:18)

And we know that God causes all things to work together for good to those who love God, to those who are called according to His purpose.

(Rom. 8:28)

fearing, trusting, and worshipping my God, whereas God allows that suffering to take place to prove to Satan that even if Satan takes all that God has blessed us with, good health, wealth, protection for us and our families, we will continue to fear, trust him, and grow spiritually through tests and trials or through discipline in order to get us back into fellowship with God and recover from our sins or backsliding.

Pastor Karabo: So your suffering was necessary?

Tumelo: Absolutely, to discipline

For it is better, if God should will it so, that you suffer for doing what is right rather than for doing what is wrong.

(1 Pet. 3:17)

Do not be deceived, God is not mocked, for whatever a man sows, this he will also reap. For the one who sows to his own flesh shall from the flesh reap corruption.

Gal. 6:7-8)

Therefore, let those also who suffer according to the will of God entrust their souls to a faithful Creator in doing what is right.

(1 Pet. 4:19)

me when I am out of fellowship or backsliding, or to bless me to grow in faith or spiritually by allowing trials and tests to strengthen my faith in God. Suffering will come and more than once for the glorification of God, not man or Satan.

Pastor Karabo: So your misfortunes worked for your good.

Tumelo: If I did not go through them, I would not have realized how far away I've gone from serving the living God.

Pastor Karabo: So you haven't stopped

It is not the healthy who need a doctor, but the sick. I have not come to call the righteous, but sinners.

(Mark 2:17)

The word of God is alive and powerful, sharper than any two edged sword, piercing even to the dividing asunder of the soul and the spirit, and of the joints and marrow, and is a critic of thoughts and intents of the heart.

(Heb. 4:12)

God helps those who need his help and not those who help themselves.

(Epigram)

doing good?

Tumelo: Pastor, this time, I have to focus on the divine good and not the human good. I have to do the right thing, the right way. I will continue to give, pray, show compassion, etc., not for me but for the glorification of God and not for my own selfish desires or to try and bribe God for selfish gains.

Pastor Karabo: God's stick has done good teaching!

Tumelo: God has made me sober!

Pastor Karabo: So it is true that suffering is the quickest diet to reduce a fat head!

Tumelo: Absolutely. It has not

For such is the will of God that by doing right you may silence the ignorance of foolish men.

(1 Pet. 2:15)

For I have learned to be content in whatever circumstances I am, I know how to get along with humble means, and I also know how to live in prosperity, in any and every circumstance I have learned the secret of being filled and going hungry, both of having abundance and suffering need. I can do all things through him who strengthens me.

(Phil. 4:11-13)

You shall receive power when the Holy Spirit has come upon you, and you shall be My witnesses.

(Acts 1:8)

come to injure me but to provide more opportunities to remind me of the presence of God.

Pastor Karabo: My son, I am proud of you, and I encourage you to study the Word of God consistently, and you will see his grace and his work at hand.

Tumelo: Grace! Grace, grace all the way!

Pastor Karabo: All the way!

Tumelo: I am even motivated to be a fisher of men and do what you have done for me, and help guide those who need the grace of God out of the darkness of sin

Doctrine in your soul, is like panacea, a cure for all, a remedy for everything.

(Epigram)

You cannot speak and think beyond your vocabulary.

(Epigram)

You shall receive power when the Holy Spirit has come upon you, and you shall be My witnesses.

and tell the unbelievers about the love of God for them, about salvation, his grace, mercy, and about God's wonderful plan for their lives and encourage the believers to continue walking by faith.

Pastor Karabo: Shall we pray? Heavenly Father, we thank you for your grace, love, mercy, and your faithfulness. We thank you for your plan for our lives. We thank Christ for executing that plan on the cross, and we thank God the Holy Spirit for revealing and teaching us about you and your plan. In Christ's name. Amen.

When the ominous clouds of uncertainty obscure our path, the radiant light of God's word pierces the darkness to illuminate our way. For such is God, Our God forever and ever, He will guide us until death.

(Ps. 48:14)

And as He was going by the sea of Galilee, He saw Simon and Andrew, the brother of Simon, casting a net in the sea, for they were fishermen. And Jesus said to them, "Follow Me and I will make you become fishers of men." And they immediately left the nets and followed him.

(Mark 1:16-18)

"Thanks be to God for His indescribable gift. Amen.

(2 Cor. 9)